INDIACOLOR

INDIACOLOR
Spirit, Tradition, and Style

Photographs by
MELBA LEVICK

Text by
MITCHELL CRITES
&
AMEETA NANJI

CHRONICLE BOOKS
SAN FRANCISCO

For Hugh, my beloved and loving partner in life and in travels. I thank you with all my heart. —ML

For my father, Sultan; my mother, Zarina; my brother, Anil; and my sister, Meena. —AN

For my wife, Niloufar, whose beauty, culture, and taste never fail to inspire and guide me. —MC

PAGES 2—3 A group of vivacious Rajasthani girls holding sickles, on their way to work in the fields on the outskirts of Jodhpur.

ABOVE An array of flower garlands and pods displayed for sale at the flower market in Varanasi.

Text copyright © 2008 by Mitchell Crites & Ameeta Nanji.
Photography copyright © 2008 by Melba Levick.
All rights reserved. No part of this book may be reproduced in any form without written permission from the publisher.

Library of Congress Cataloging-in-Publication Data available.

ISBN: 978-0-8118-5316-3

Manufactured in China.
Design by Laura Bagnato.
Photo selection and layout by Melba Levick.

10 9 8 7 6 5 4 3 2 1

Chronicle Books LLC
680 Second Street
San Francisco, California 94107
www.chroniclebooks.com

CONTENTS

INTRODUCTION

India is a land of vibrant color. Color is an integral part of the lifestyle in India. It is part of religious rituals, cultural activities, and daily routines, and is found everywhere from clothing and customs to foods and festivals. Ayurvedic healers associate colors with the seven main chakras, energy centers located in the human body along the spinal column. Each chakra has a dominant color: red for the root chakra (located at the perineum), yellow for the navel, green for the heart, and so on. Surya, the personification of the sun, is often depicted in a chariot drawn by seven horses representing the colors of the rainbow.

Indian bazaars sizzle with color. Vendors' containers brim with deep red and orange powders for social and religious rituals. In the Hindu tradition, colored pigment has an essential role in daily life. It is used in many ways, from the *bindu* (seed)—which devotees place on the *ajna* chakra (between the eyebrows), considered the seat of latent wisdom—to the smearing of ritual color on temple deities. In a daily ritual, men throughout India place red vermilion powder on their wives' foreheads and the parting of their hair as a sign of *saubhagya* (happiness). The visual impact of color is inescapable wherever you turn. Splashes of color turn up at a village well as women wearing flowing *odhinis* (veils) fetch water, or in the whirling luster of a dancer's skirt sewn with glittering mirrors. Iridescent greens and blues of peacocks, mustard-field yellows, and pinks of perfumed rose petals abound in India.

India is made up of many different worlds, and among these is the realm of color, pattern, and design, spanning thousands of years and spreading across the length and breadth of the country. Indian design and craft are based in traditions that have seeped, taken root and spread through time and through generations in music and dance, ritual and prayer, painting, weaving, carving, and architecture. The origins of these artistic traditions are varied and come from within the many cultures and faiths that share the history of India; from the seasons; and from the earth, water, and natural resources. The omnipresent decoration has its roots in ritual, connecting people to a greater tradition. Whether to invoke and propitiate deities, exorcise negative forces, celebrate rites of passage, or mark turning points in the cycle of death and renewal, ritual creates a focus. It transforms all areas of life from the mundane and ordinary to the sacred and inspired.

India's streets are a melting pot of her culture. People take to the streets on every important religious and social occasion. As the brief season of spring warms the atmosphere, northern India cuts loose for a day of fun and frolic. Holi, the festival of color, is celebrated on the day after the full moon in early March. Clouds of pink, green, and turquoise *gulal* (bright-colored powders traditionally made from medicinal herbs) fill the air, and streets are turned into chaos with dance and song. Originally a festival to celebrate good harvests and fertility of the land, today Holi is an excuse for people to shed their inhibitions and caste differences for a day of spring fever. Teenagers spend the day flirting and misbehaving in the streets, adults extend the hand of peace, and people chase each other around, tossing gulal over each other.

In today's India, newborn modernity rubs shoulders with living history; domes and minarets of four-hundred-year-old Mughal relics share the skyline with modern highways. Dusty, rickety outdoor markets are neighbors to gleaming glass shopping malls. As you plunge into the crowded, medieval, labyrinthine streets of the old section of any big town in India you will see the same types of jewels, spices, and brocades that have been sold in those very places for hundreds of years. Cows block the path of SUVs, and at night men chat and smoke bidis under the stars while the in-crowd grooves to techno-*bangra* (Punjabi folk music) beats in a bar around the corner. But to mingle only with the well-heeled is to miss out on the teeming, age-old commotion of India's streets, including brightly painted auto-rickshaws, flower-garland sellers, painted elephants, mischievous monkeys, colorful sari shops, bangle bazaars, *mehndi* (henna) artists, and street musicians and performers.

India has approximately sixteen official languages, thousands of dialects, several of the world's great religions, and a population of more than one billion. With a history that traces back to settlements on the Indus River nearly five thousand years ago, India has been invaded, conquered, and subjugated since the days of Alexander the Great. It became a modern nation-state in 1947, when the British partitioned the former empire into the new countries of India and Pakistan. Unlike the ancient civilizations of Egypt and Greece, whose contributions to world history have been relegated to museums and monuments, India has been able to carry on evolving her traditions, despite having been conquered and dominated by foreign invaders.

Even in the face of such invasions, art and craft remain integral to Indian life. Artisans and craftspeople are tucked away in narrow lanes of the largest cities and in the remotest villages. Hearing the whirr of a shuttle flying across a handloom, the resonant tap-tap of a stone carver shaping a white marble Lakshmi (goddess of abundance), or a metalsmith molding a copper urn is an everyday experience as you take a stroll through a bazaar or a distant rural village.

While remaining true to the country's own artistic traditions, Indian culture has also absorbed and adapted myriad stylistic influences. Across the span of several centuries, Mughal design style has transformed northern Indian architecture. Mughal decorative techniques, used in carved and pierced stone often inlaid with mirror or colored glass, were embraced and developed by Indian craftspeople. This can be seen clearly in the *havelis* (townhouses of wealthy merchants), palaces, and forts all over northwest India. Samode Bagh, a hundred-and-fifty-year-old garden outside Jaipur, has been influenced greatly by the Mughal *char-bagh*, Persian-style gardens. Samode Bagh is surrounded

PAGE 6 Carefully tied glass bangles piled high in the Jaipur bangle bazaar.

PAGE 7 A Rajasthani musician displaying his mustache at a fair in Jaipur.

OPPOSITE TOP Veiled young women in the village of Delwaran, Rajasthan.

OPPOSITE BOTTOM Langur monkeys groom each other on the steps of a Jain temple in Ranakpur, Rajasthan.

BELOW The Peacock Man, Kali Charan Singh, selling feathers for good luck inside the historic Jaisalmer Fort.

RIGHT Detail of an embroidered Rajasthani skirt.

LEFT Two Rajasthani women in a village on the outskirts of Jaipur.

BELOW TOP Colored powders for Holi, the festival of colors, displayed at a fair in Jaipur.

BELOW BOTTOM A Rajasthani goatherd dressed in traditional clothes and jewelry.

by luxuriant green lawns and flowering trees and crisscrossed with reflecting pools, gently rippling fountains, and water channels.

Walls embellished with colorful paintings are a frequent sight in India. In classical texts like the *Kama Sutra* of Vatsyana, painting is considered one of the sixty-four fine arts. Other treatises, namely the *Shilparatna* and the *Manasollasa*, provide detailed methods of preparing walls, plasters, and colors for murals. Color—for dyeing cloth, for painting miniatures and walls, for tossing in the air in festivals and worship—comes from the earth. Colors are made from minerals, vegetables, indigo, conch shells, and pure gold and silver. The preparing and mixing of colors is an elaborate process that takes weeks or sometimes months to produce the desired results.

Semiprecious and precious stones, rich in color, are used in jewelry and carry deep meanings. For example, according to Hindu astrology, nine celestial bodies are represented by particular precious stones. Navratan, a particular combination of nine jewels strung or set together, is believed to ensure abundant wealth, happiness, longevity, honor, and mental peace for the wearer. Navratan comprises ruby (sun), white pearl (moon), red coral (Mars), emerald (Mercury), yellow sapphire (Jupiter), diamond (Venus), blue sapphire (Saturn), garnet (Rahu), and cat's eye (Ketu). (Rahu and Ketu were considered by the ancients to be sensitive nodal points created by the intersection of the moon's orbit with the ecliptic at two places.) Gold and silver also hold an important meaning, symbolizing the sacred rivers Ganga and Yamuna. Extracted from the earth, these same jewels that are carved and polished by artisans and set into magnificent jewelry are also ground and made into pigments used by artists.

Even cities are identified in legend and memory with color. Jaipur, the Pink City, is dotted with rosy terra-cotta extracted from the grinding of red sandstone from nearby quarries, perhaps to connect and evoke the grandeur of the Mughal monuments of Agra and Delhi. Color plays an essential role in the purple-blue of the houses of Jodhpur, the Blue City; the golden sandstone of Jaisalmer, the Golden City; the white-washed havelis, palaces, and pavilions of pleasure of Udaipur, the White City; and the dark red, intricately carved stone of Bikaner.

The roots of the intense creativity found in every aspect of life in India lie in its rich traditions and dynamic history. Indian artists and craftspeople, creating artwork ranging from tribal to classical, continue to surprise with their originality, imagination, resourcefulness, skill, and, most of all, their sense of joy.

Today, though free from foreign invasions, India is being transformed by the rush of the modern world and by confronting the problems that come with industrial civilization. Despite the hardships that the majority of the population endures, there is an undeniable, enigmatic spirit of joy that prevails, especially in the people of rural India—perhaps because people in the countryside lead simple lives, owning hardly anything. Paradoxically, India is one of the fastest-growing economies in the world. The country now faces the challenge of coping with the effects of modernization while protecting its environment and preserving its spirit and culture.

After many millennia of Indian civilization, the human spirit continues to express itself through rituals, art and music, color, and endless varieties of patterns and styles. This irrepressible spirit not only thrives here but also serves as an infinite source of inspiration for people all over the world.

DOORS & PASSAGES

In the architecture of India, the zones of transition from one space to another often have a deep and profound meaning. The mud-packed walls of a village hut may be plain, but the doors are beautifully carved and painted. In addition, the threshold of a house may indicate the wealth and status of the owner and also give clues to the religion, caste, or community to which the family belongs.

In Hindu homes, thresholds and doors are regularly anointed with colored lacquer and powder, which ensure that the dwelling and its inhabitants will be protected and blessed by the gods. The highly auspicious image of Lord Ganesh, the elephant god, who is also considered the remover of obstacles, is traditionally installed in a niche above the entrance doorway.

The grandest and most highly decorated doors are normally found in temples, haveli courtyard homes, royal forts, and palaces. Rich merchants and hereditary rulers commissioned the finest master artisans in their kingdoms to design and create the entrance gateways and doors to their fortified palaces, which often rise above the merely functional and reach the level of major works of art.

The materials, decorative techniques, and designs used in the creation of doors and passages are rich and varied. Ornamental doors are carved from a variety of hardwoods including teak, mahogany, ebony, and rosewood. To enhance their beauty, they are painted, gilded, enameled, inlaid with ivory, or covered with silver sheet. Floral and geometric designs and auspicious symbols are commonly used, as are animal and human figures drawn from mythology and heroic epic tales.

Inside traditional palaces, the complexities of ritual and court life slowly unfold as visitors wind their way through labyrinthine passages. They begin in the public rooms and pass through beautiful doors and narrow corridors into the secluded *zenana*, the apartments of the queen and her attendants, on into sumptuous pavilions of pleasure, private temples, and magnificent throne rooms where the maharaja once sat in state on a gold and jeweled throne. The visitors' passage from light to dark, public to private, and female to male is a remarkable journey in itself.

PAGE 12 Chand Pol, the Gate of the Moon, provides the principal western entrance into Fort Neemrana. The majestic gateway, with its massive, iron-spiked doors, was built to discourage charging elephants during enemy invasions. The scalloped frame of the archway is covered with faded floral paintings.

PAGE 13 A grand arched corridor inside Fort Neemrana leads to the Gate of the Moon. At dusk, its thick stone walls are bathed in golden sunlight and shadow.

ABOVE AND OPPOSITE These four famous doors inside the private apartments of the Jaipur City Palace are carved and painted in the shape of a peacock, with its magnificent fanlike tail. They represent four important seasons of the Indian calendar, which is traditionally divided into six periods.

The Solar Door (**OPPOSITE LEFT**) represents the early winter season and is painted with the image of the sun. The elegant wooden door panels, framed in white marble, are carved with images of fruit and flowers and covered with hammered brass sheet. Stylized red poppies are depicted on each side of the door, and a spreading peacock tail, rendered in shades of green, blue, and tarnished silver, fills the curving space of the upper wall.

Flanked by two guardian figures, the Lotus Door (**OPPOSITE RIGHT**) derives its name from the array of pink lotus flowers that entwine the entire threshold and upper wall. This exquisite door is traditionally associated with spring.

The subtle patterns of the Green Door (**ABOVE LEFT**) evoke autumn, when the mountains and hills around Jaipur remain lush and verdant after the monsoon rains.

The Peacock Door (**ABOVE RIGHT**) is sculpted in relief with the images of five majestic peacocks painted in indigo and iridescent green. It symbolizes the monsoon season, when the male peacocks spread their tails in a ritual mating dance of great beauty.

OPPOSITE LEFT Framed by white marble columns and an arch carved with lotus blossoms, this splendid door inside the palace apartments at the Bikaner Junagadh Fort is painted with floral patterns in the traditional desert palette of orange, green, and gold.

OPPOSITE RIGHT The door frame of this royal temple, high in the private apartments of the Kuchaman Fort, is adorned with newly restored images of Lord Krishna and his adoring female devotees. Traces of original paint can still be found at the base of the wooden door, which has been pierced with a lotus blossom pattern.

LEFT Once the residence of the finance minister for the desert kingdom of Jaisalmer, the recently converted Hotel Suraj retains much of its original painting and architectural detail. This carved door from one of the bedroom suites has been ritually anointed by the owner with red ocher so that the property and its inhabitants may be protected and blessed.

ABOVE It has become the trend in recent years to rejuvenate plain, old doors by painting them with floral designs, animals, or images drawn from the rich epic literature of Rajasthan. On the panels of this newly painted door, aristocratic lovers meet, perhaps secretly, in a tree-lined garden filled with flowers.

chapter
2

ADORNMENT

Embellishment and adornment play an essential role in the culture of India. As the sun rises, women in homes ranging from village hut to urban apartment quietly drape themselves in saris, which have been woven and dyed in an endless array of patterns and colors, choose matching bangles, and apply the *tikka* dot or streak of colored powder to their foreheads. On festival days they painstakingly draw swirling patterns of henna paste, known as *mehndi*, on their hands and feet, staining them vermilion red.

In the countryside, color and embellishment are everywhere—on clothing, vehicles, even animals. Men wear colorful turbans, a stylish way for them to indicate where they come from and protect their heads from the heat of the sun. The shepherd marks his livestock with daubs of colorful paint so that he can identify them easily if any of his flock should stray. Working camels have their coats painted and trimmed to create light and dark cameo-like patterns, and the trunks and bodies of elephants that carry tourists up to the Amber Palace are ornamented with bright-colored flowers and traditional symbols.

Nowhere is animal adornment more prevalent than at the many animal fairs held around the country, and one of the most famous is at Pushkar. Visitors from all over India and abroad come to see the camel races and folk dancing and to enjoy the festive atmosphere. Buying and selling of livestock is the order of the day, and owners are busy grooming, painting, and decorating their camels, horses, cattle, and donkeys in order to fetch the highest price.

Truck and scooter drivers take great pride in embellishing their vehicles with foiled tinsel and satin ribbons, which blow in the wind. Pithy proverbs, poems, and warnings against ill health or bad fortune adorn vehicles, and spotting them on a long road journey becomes a delightful way to pass the time. Messages glimpsed on trucks and scooters might include "No life without wife," "If you give me the evil eye, your face will blacken," "Work is worship," "Love begets love," "Drive carefully; remember who goes with you," and, summing it all up, "Life is a stage. We are actors and God is the Director."

PAGE 18 The front of this truck is brightly painted and decked out with garlands, tinsel, and ribbons. Known as "queens of the highway," these festooned trucks are among the brightest and most striking sights on the busy roads of India.

PAGE 19 The back of this moving wagon opens up to reveal a portable shrine honoring several Hindu gods and goddesses.

LEFT Villagers who live near the main roads and highways carry on a thriving business by making garlands and tinsel hangings for the decoration of trucks, tractors, and scooters.

ABOVE A driver stops to "freshen up" his tractor adding yet another layer of adornment, a common practice, especially on festival days.

OPPOSITE TOP Each major town has an area where artists specialize in the painting and decoration of trucks and buses. Drivers can choose the designs and motifs they want, which can range from peacocks to Bollywood movie stars. Here, a truck has been outfitted with an intricate pastel design.

OPPOSITE CENTER The words "Horn please" appear on most trucks on Indian roads, and the honking of horns is frequently heard as drivers prepare to pass. A recently spotted sign on another truck was a lesson in humility: "Don't Forget Your Humanity."

OPPOSITE BOTTOM Indian truck drivers take great pride in their vehicles. The front of a truck is brightly painted and decked out with garlands, tinsel, and ribbon. Known as "queens of the highway," these festooned trucks are among the brightest and most striking sights on the busy roads of India.

ABOVE A roadside stall offers scalloped curtain valances for sale, used both to decorate vehicles and to shade drivers' eyes from the glaring sun.

RIGHT Three-wheel scooters are the main mode of transport in many small Indian towns. The proud driver of this scooter hasn't left an inch of his vehicle undecorated.

ABOVE TOP The Pushkar animal fair, held in central Rajasthan each autumn, attracts visitors from all over India and abroad. Camel racing, tribal dance performances, and the brisk trade in livestock (desert camels, donkeys, cows, horses, and even the odd water buffalo) make this one of the liveliest and most festive events in India.

Stalls selling handmade animal regalia spring up everywhere at the Pushkar fair. Harnesses, beaded necklaces, ear pom-poms, tooled saddles, and anklets sewn with tiny bells are all on display. Owners compete with each other in the art of grooming and ornamenting their favorite camels.

ABOVE BOTTOM AND RIGHT Camel owners paint their animals from head to tail with a variety of geometric and floral patterns using bold black paint. The distinctive designs identify as well as beautify the animals. Rose-shaped red pom-poms are used to ornament the camel's nose while traditional necklaces strung with cowrie shells, colored buttons, beads, and bells are hung from the neck.

OPPOSITE LEFT Richly caparisoned with a mirrored crown and embroidered trappings, a white horse is ready to carry a groom to a tented wedding pavilion, where his bride and the guests await.

CENTER He may be a working donkey, but his owner has taken time to carefully dress him up with a headdress of orange flowers.

ABOVE Sporting a rainbow-colored patchwork saddle and draped with beaded necklaces and pom-poms, this noble camel greets visitors when they arrive at the Rambagh Palace in Jaipur.

OPPOSITE AND ABOVE These tame and
friendly elephants are painted by their keepers,
whose families have been looking after the
magnificent beasts for centuries. They patiently
ferry tourists up to the hilltop fortress of Amber,
the original capital of Jaipur. Lakshmi, decorated
with a star on her forehead, and her daughter,
Shakuntala, adorned with red pom-poms in her
ears, stand together for a formal portrait on the
banks of the Jal Mahal Lake near Amber.

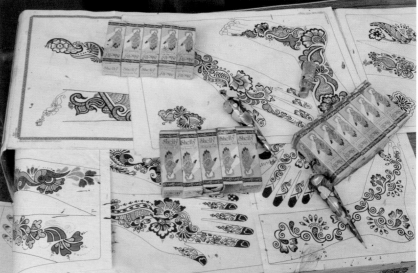

LEFT AND ABOVE Elaborate tattoolike designs (*mehndi*) are traditionally painted on the palms of a bride's hands and on the soles of her feet as part of the marriage ceremony. Girls often get together and paint each other's hands and feet during Diwali, the festival of light, and other Indian holidays as well. To save time, ready-made stencils are sometimes used. The red stain is not permanent and gradually wears off over a period of several weeks.

31

ABOVE AND RIGHT Mehndi designs are limited only by the creativity of the maker. These intricate patterns adorned the hands of a group of women on their way to a wedding near the Agra Fort.

FLOWERS

Legends about flowers abound in India, and beautiful gardens and flowers provide an essential background for the stories of Krishna, one of the most popular gods in the Hindu pantheon. According to mythology, Raat Ki Rani (Queen of the Night) is a heavenly tree that was brought to earth by Lord Krishna. A jealous quarrel ensued between Krishna's two wives, Satyabhama and Rukmini, over who would get the tree. To appease them both, mischievous Krishna planted this tree in Satyabhama's courtyard, but just on the edge, so that when the tree flowered the blooms fell  in Rukmini's garden. In another story, this one telling of the origin of night-blooming jasmine, Parijataka fell in love with Surya (the sun god), but when he deserted her, she killed herself and a tree sprung from the ashes. Unable to stand the sight of the lover who left her, the tree flowers only at night and sheds its blossoms like teardrops before the sun rises.

Trees, plants, and flowers are worshipped in India. The Nandavanas (sacred groves) were considered the abode of the gods, dedicated especially to the mother goddess, with all the trees, plants, and flowers in the grove grown as an offering to her. These ancient groves were essentially small botanical gardens, including many local plant and flower species. In these groves were ponds in which grew medicinal plants and flowers essential to Ayurveda (science of life).

Flowers, the jewels of the botanical world, carry potent messages in India. A simple jasmine flower held in the hand, or a garland of marigolds placed around the neck, speaks a universal language, straight from the heart. An important part of a marriage ceremony is the ritual of the garlands, when the bride and bridegroom exchange garlands strung with roses, jasmine, and tuberoses; the fragrant blooms represent the natural world bearing witness to the union of two souls, who are placing a circle of protection around each other.

Not reserved just for special occasions, buying flowers every day is a long tradition in India. Flowers are plentiful in India; the front of a brightly painted transport truck is often festooned with marigolds for good luck on its journey, marigolds adorn many a roadside shrine, and delicately woven strings of jasmine decorate a woman's hair. The finest floral hair ornaments cost only a few rupees and lend a touch of elegance to everyday life.

PAGE 34 In Delhi, a young flower seller nimbly weaves marigold garlands heaped up in a cane basket.

PAGE 35 A flower seller sits on a sidewalk with her basket of fresh marigolds in Delhi.

ABOVE A riot of color: garlands of roses, marigolds, and jasmine overflow a cane basket outside a temple in Udaipur, Rajasthan.

RIGHT A flower seller outside Jagdish Temple in Udaipur, Rajasthan, sells flowers to devotees who will offer them to the temple deities.

FAR RIGHT A vendor displays a garland of fresh roses in the Jaipur flower bazaar.

LEFT Splashes of color adorn the flower bazaar in Jodhpur, Rajasthan, as flower sellers wearing red and pink veils sell marigolds in bamboo cane baskets.

ABOVE A traditionally dressed Rajasthani gentleman uses marigolds to decorate the entrance of Fateh Bagh, a Ranakpur heritage hotel.

LEFT Elaborate garlands of roses, marigolds, and jasmine are among the floral offerings for sale in the flower bazaar in Varanasi, Uttar Pradesh.

BOTTOM Iris garlands displayed for sale in the flower bazaar in Varanasi.

OPPOSITE Flowers strung into never-ending garlands are cut to the customers' desired length.

BAZAAR

Since long before Marco Polo passed through India on the Silk Route to China in the thirteenth century, visitors have been bewitched and bedazzled by the fabled bazaars of India. In diaries and chronicles, travelers have described in great detail the extraordinary spice markets, where saffron, black pepper, cinnamon, and cardamom were bought and transported by ship and overland caravan to the Western marketplace. The quantities of precious textiles, spices, and other goods exported to the ancient world were so great that they caused the economy of the Roman Empire to become severely strained.

Today, the descendants of those same artisans, weavers, and carvers who produced goods for the Western markets, are still creating beautiful works of art, and the bazaars across India are bursting with an incredible array of things to buy. One of the busiest and most colorful bazaars in India can be found in Jaipur, the capital of Rajasthan, the Land of Kings. The Jaipur bazaar, once it opens at mid-morning, teems with customers throughout the day until closing time, around nine or ten at night.

The broad, arcaded streets and narrow lanes of Jaipur are filled with locals and tourists. Certain areas are famous for the wonderful handcrafted goods made and sold there. On the Street of the Marble Workers near the Gate of the Moon, you can find carved white marble statues of gods and goddesses, the figure of a favorite grandparent, or even a beloved pet immortalized in stone. The lacquer and glass bangle bazaar always attracts a great deal of attention from ladies of all ages. Nearby in the Choti Chaupar square, flower sellers string jasmine, rose, and marigold blossoms into garlands that will adorn the deities of the hundreds of active temples scattered around the city. And gleaming brass and copper pots and utensils are piled high in the Tripoliya Bazaar, just outside the magnificent city palace, where the maharaja of Jaipur still lives.

Merchandise prices on any given street can range from fifty cents to fifty thousand dollars. Go early in the morning to be the first customer of the day, and bargain hard—the merchants expect it. Keep in mind that shopkeepers consider it an inauspicious start to the day if they don't succeed in making a sale to the first customer of the morning. So, if you arrive early, chances are you'll get what you fancy at the price you want.

PAGE 40 Deep inside the Jodhpur central market, these women are selling locally made tie-dyed material. Many of the houses and public spaces in the city have been painted in shades of blue, an expression of the longing for water in this desert kingdom.

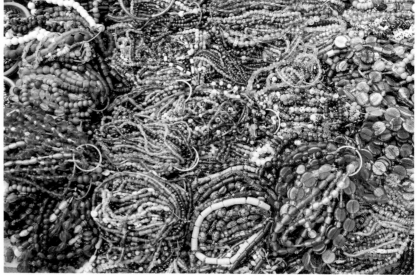

PAGE 41, OPPOSITE, AND THIS PAGE The great Indian bazaar has something for everybody. Many items are still crafted by hand by traditional artisans. These images of bazaars across India show the wide range of products available at these festive markets, including tie-dyed costumes, painted and gilded glass lamps, hand-bound ledger books, beaded glass necklaces, brass and copper utensils, silver-foiled sweets to nibble on while you shop, and even pitchforks crafted out of bentwood.

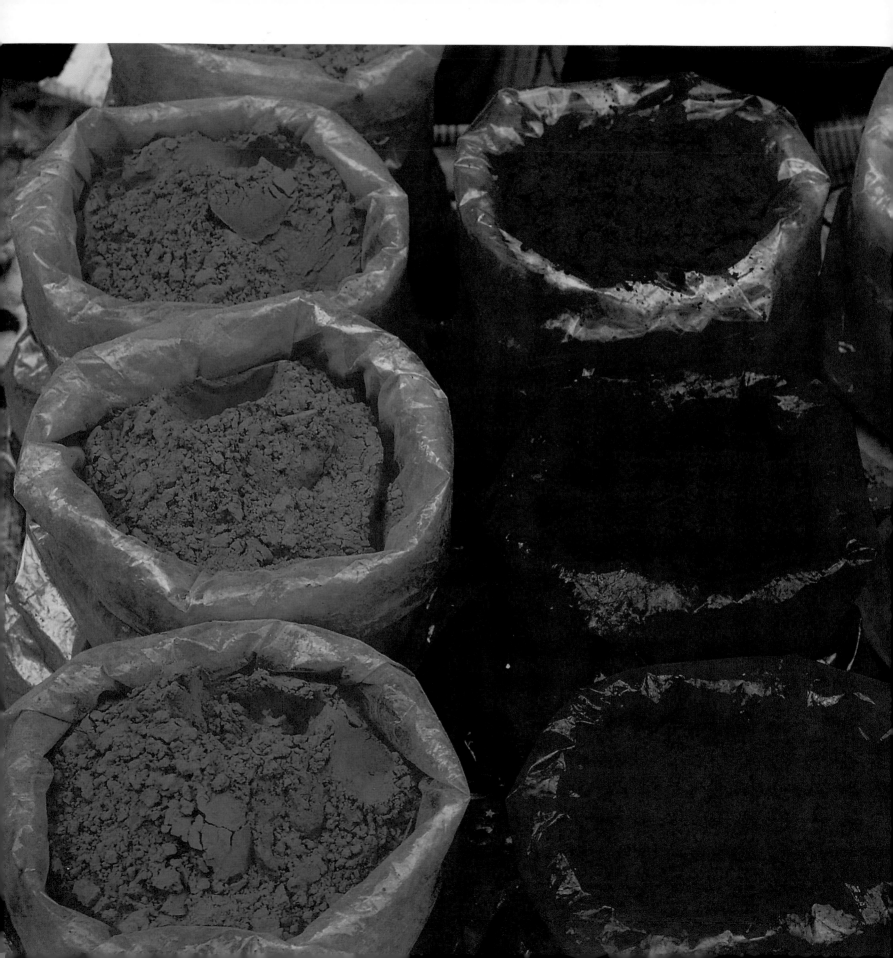

LEFT Sold from open bags, these bright-colored powders are thrown wildly in the air during the ritual celebration of Holi, the Hindu festival of color.

ABOVE Host to hundreds of thousands of tourists who visit each year, the busy market streets of Varanasi are best explored by bicycle rickshaw.

OPPOSITE AND THIS PAGE Handmade shoes, slippers, and sandals are among the most popular items in Indian bazaars. Traditional cobblers stitch the footwear using leather and fabric, which is then embroidered or embellished with sequins and colored glass beads. Each region of India has its own distinctive style of footwear that is instantly recognizable to the connoisseur.

OPPOSITE TOP Many varieties of grains, seeds, and legumes, such as lentils, chickpeas, and peanuts, are sold in the dried produce markets. They make delicious snacks and are used in many Indian dishes.

OPPOSITE BOTTOM Traditional fried snacks like *panipuri* and potato *tikkis* are prepared fresh and sold in the bazaar.

RIGHT Small open stalls are set up every day on the Varanasi *ghats* (steps leading down to water), where thousands of pilgrims pass on their way to bathe in the holy waters of the Ganges.

BELOW Trying to tempt tourists with his selection of religious cloths and flowers, this determined merchant floats in his boat up and down the banks of the Ganges at Varanasi.

ANIMALS EVERYWHERE

Animals are everywhere in India—in fields, temples, villages, towns, and big cities. It is not unusual to walk down the street and have to maneuver around several cows calmly standing or sitting in the median of a busy road. Cows, monkeys, and pigs share the streets with dogs, donkeys, and the occasional camel carrying goods to market. It is arguably the only place in the world where you will see elephants and camels vying with buses and cars for the right of way. Then there is the small town of Pushkar, in Rajasthan, which has gained international recognition as the venue of the largest camel fair in the world. Though the festival is known primarily for its camel trade, it has become a lively meeting ground for travelers from all over the world, nomadic musicians and performers, and traders of cattle, horses, sheep, and goats.

Since ancient times, Indians have recognized the animals' right to coexist with human beings. Animals were loved, nurtured, and even worshipped, and they were given the status of gods and goddesses. Even today, they are depicted as the mode of transportation of gods and goddesses; Varuna, the rain god, rides on Makara, the crocodile, and Ganesh, the remover of obstacles, is often shown riding on a rat. The concept of *goshala*, a place where cows are sheltered, was originally introduced in Jainism, an ancient philosophy whose main emphasis is on *ahimsa*, or nonviolence.

The belief in the dignity and value of animals is also evident in Indian literature. The two-thousand-year-old *Panchatantra* includes a collection of animal stories and is considered to be the basis for *Aesop's Fables*. The *Garudapurana* (ancient texts of Garuda, the bird god) contains life histories of eagles, fish, and turtles. Several religious texts are dedicated to specific animals, such as the *Nagamahdimya* (writings on snake worship) and *Nandi-purdoa* (writings on the worship of cows). Although some of these texts date back more than five thousand years, their themes are extremely relevant today, with messages about protecting and conserving the earth's delicate ecosystem, the cycles of nature, and environmental ecology. These ideals of conservation, compassion, and nonviolence are beneficial not only to animals but also to humans and, indeed, the entire earth. What the authors of these ancient texts seem to be saying is that what is good for animals is good for all of us.

PAGE 50 A young white zebu (also known as a "Brahma cow") appears to be part of the architecture as she walks past a building through one of the narrow alleys inside the Jaisalmer Fort, Rajasthan.

PAGE 51 A gray langur monkey sits on a low wall eating sugarcane at the Ranakpur Temple in Rajasthan.

LEFT A camel transports a load of hay as his turbaned master walks beside him on the way to Khimsar, Rajasthan.

ABOVE A *mahout* (elephant keeper) stands on the trunk of his brightly painted elephant on the road to Amber Palace, on the outskirts of Jaipur.

OPPOSITE TOP A Brahma bull (with its characteristic hump) walks through the streets of Jaipur, Rajasthan.

OPPOSITE BOTTOM A goat perches on a ledge in one of the narrow streets within the fort at Jaisalmer, Rajasthan.

ABOVE A street in Jaipur becomes a gathering place for cows and a pregnant pig.

OPPOSITE TOP Camels bask in the sun at the Pushkar Camel Fair, held every November during the week of the full moon. Camels are decorated with woven colored yarn belts and straps, colorful tassels, buttons, bells, and jingling anklets on their feet.

OPPOSITE BOTTOM A herd of cows enjoys the warmth of the sun on the banks of the River Ganges, Varanasi.

ABOVE Nomadic goatherds wearing the deep-red turbans that are characteristic of the Rabari community walk their goats to grazing pastures.

RIGHT A young goatherd brings her goats home at sunset in the desert sand dunes near Khimsar, Rajasthan.

WOMEN AT WORK

Women in rural India have a powerful connection with water, for it is their traditional role to fetch and carry water from the village well. Clad in brilliant red, pink, and orange veils, groups of women fill their water pots. They place one or even two heavy clay or metal pots on their heads and wind their way back home; their long arms, like the necks of swans, curve sensuously around the bellies of their pots. Rural Indian women are known for their ease of movement, long necks, straight and slender backs, and stylish stances. A seemingly idyllic life. The reality, however, is that in some places women spend up to six hours a day bringing water to their homes from the wells. Despite these hardships, their close relationship with water has made women experts on conserving and maintaining the quality of this life-giving resource.

Rural women and girls are involved in many other areas of work. They prepare cooking fuel by mixing dung with twigs and fodder from crops. They take care of the female animals, grazing them in the fields, cleaning them and their sheds, milking them, and feeding them. They collect food, building materials, and wood and grass for their houses, and gather and administer medicinal plants.

In many remote rural areas, women who work as brick makers are bound to their employers through contracts like those used for serfs. Other women migrate to big cities looking for work and are often employed as day laborers at construction sites. A common sight is that of women vigorously digging a ditch, but dressed to the nines in colorful *ghaghras* (gathered skirts), *cholis* (short blouses), and *odhinis* (veils); they will often be wearing shining silver bangles on their arms, silver anklets flashing beneath their flowery skirt pleats, *husslis* (chokers) around their necks, and earrings dangling from their lobes. Their grace is always evident as they work under even the harshest conditions.

Progress is on the horizon for Indian women. Some have started forest protection movements; women in India were the first to hug trees to prevent lumber companies from chopping them down. In an effort to gain financial and social recognition, rural women, especially in Gujarat, have organized themselves, with the help of private groups, into an important economic force. And now rural women are opening and managing their own bank accounts.

PAGE 58 A woman near Jaisalmer, Rajasthan, carefully transfers valuable water from one clay pot to another for her family's use.

PAGE 59 An urban woman rides a scooter in Udaipur, Rajasthan, having covered herself from top to toe to protect herself from traffic fumes.

LEFT AND OPPOSITE BOTTOM Women weave bamboo cane baskets in their homes, in an area of Jodhpur, Rajasthan, that has become known as the bamboo bazaar. Men and women share the task of weaving these baskets, which are used largely to transport and store agricultural produce.

OPPOSITE TOP LEFT A brick maker pushes a wheelbarrow at a brick factory between Agra and Jaipur.

OPPOSITE TOP RIGHT Two women make dots of brilliant color as they lay out handmade paper to dry in the sun in Sanganer, on the outskirts of Jaipur, one of the main papermaking centers of Rajasthan.

LEFT A woman at the Pushkar Camel Fair collects cow dung that has been mixed with straw and patted into flat circular shapes to be used as fuel for cooking and heating in villages.

BELOW Colorfully dressed women near Delhi collect cooking fuel, a mixture of cow dung and straw, for loading on to a truck bound for village markets, where it will be sold.

OPPOSITE TOP Near Delhi, a railroad worker waits for the train to pass so she can lift the barrier gate.

OPPOSITE BOTTOM Women workers package salt at a salt mill outside Jodhpur.

OPPOSITE A woman tends her water buffalo in the village of Samode, Rajasthan.

RIGHT Near Ranakpur, Rajasthan, a young girl minds two oxen yoked to a horizontal wheel as they walk around in circles to draw water from an underground source. This water-wheel method of collecting water and irrigating land using animals dates back to the twelfth century.

BELOW A young Rabari girl, dressed in traditional clothes and silver jewelry, helps to tend her family's goats in Rajasthan.

OPPOSITE TOP LEFT A Rajasthani woman dressed in a red *bandhani odhini* (tie-dyed veil) carries water in a decorated clay pot.

OPPOSITE TOP RIGHT A young girl in Rajasthan balances two water pots, one clay and the other metal, on her head.

OPPOSITE BOTTOM A group of women collect water at a well near Ranakpur, Rajasthan.

ABOVE A woman washes clothes at a *ghat* (stairway leading to a water landing) at Lake Pichola in Udaipur, Rajasthan.

ABOVE A young girl and a veiled woman in a green odhini are practically camouflaged in the lush green countryside, in Delwara, Rajasthan.

OPPOSITE Women carry loads of fodder to feed their animals and to mix with cow dung for use as cooking fuel outside Jodhpur, Rajasthan.

DHURRIES
woven wonders

In the *Atharva Veda*, an ancient Sanskrit text, day and night are depicted as two sisters weaving, with the warp symbolizing darkness and the weft representing the light of day. The sacred place where the threads meet is illustrated in many hymns of the *Vedas*, and the beauty of that sacred meeting can be seen in the bright colors and bold patterns of the dhurrie.

For centuries, dhurries (flat-woven rugs) were widely used as floor coverings in the Indian subcontinent, and today they are gaining a cultlike following in the West. Their striking colors, powerful simplicity, and variety of designs provide the perfect complement to many modern interiors.

Dhurries play an important role in India's cultural history, since the floor was where most social interactions took place. Originally used by villagers for protection against heat and cold, dhurries were woven out of camel and goat hair (although now they are woven mostly with cotton, to accommodate modern urbanites who find the animal hairs too coarse). Despite its utilitarian origins, the dhurrie soon became known for its ornamental qualities. In the late eighteenth century, royal Rajasthani families recognized its beauty and functionality and began using dhurries to cover and decorate the expansive stone floors of their palaces. But soon, despite royal commissions, the craft of dhurrie weaving seemed to be in danger of disappearing. Its revival came from an unexpected source—the confines of British Raj jails. Over the years, inmates of these jails produced a wide variety of dhurries ranging from coarse and basic to some of the finest examples of traditional and innovative designs that are now sought by dhurrie collectors all over the world. These include traditional prayer rugs, dhurries with classic stripes and ornamental designs, as well as beautiful pictorial weaves. It is said that the promotion of the craft of dhurrie weaving in the Raj jails led to its renaissance, as well as to the rehabilitation of the inmates.

Today, the dhurrie is a popular floor covering used in interior spaces and verandas. Dhurries are woven in a variety of geometrical designs, stripes, and Mughal flower motifs. Their striking stripe design is achieved by warp-sharing techniques such as dovetailing and interlocking. Colors range from pastel shades of sand and duck-egg blue to the brightest of primary hues.

PAGE 70 Chemical-dyed cotton yarns lie next to a wooden fork tool used for weaving a dhurrie. Today's dhurries are smooth, light, flat-woven rugs—the perfect floor coverings during long, hot summers.

PAGE 71 A weaver at Ranakpur, Rajasthan, creates a cotton dhurrie, using wooden tools and a variety of chemical-dyed yarns that last longer than the vegetable-dyed type. "Vegetable dyes were used originally," says the weaver, "but how can we send our rugs abroad if the colors fade away?"

ABOVE A skilled artisan weaves a colorful cotton dhurrie. Weavers sit beside hand looms in villages, creating geometric and floral patterns in an exciting combination of bright as well as pastel colors.

OPPOSITE TOP A weaver in Ranakpur, Rajasthan, takes a break with her baby and pet goat.

OPPOSITE BOTTOM Shown here are a variety of cotton and camel-hair dhurries that have gone through many stages of development, from the selection and dyeing of yarn to weaving, washing, and finishing.

TEXTILES
threads of time

According to a traditional tale, Emperor Aurangzeb flew into a rage when one day he saw his daughter, Princess Zeb-un-Nissa, clad in what appeared to be nearly nothing. On being severely rebuked, the princess explained that she was wearing not just one but seven *jamahs* (dresses). Such was the fine quality of hand-woven fabrics.

As this tale indicates, high-quality weaving is a major source of pride in India. The country's textile history goes back to more than four thousand years ago, starting with the people of the Indus River Valley, who learned to transform a ball of white, fluffy cotton into fabric. This was the beginning of India's textile heritage. Ancient dyeing processes were used as far back as 300 B.C., when plants, insects, roots, and other elements from nature were used to create the basic textile color palette.

There is hardly a village in India where weavers, dyers, and printers do not exist. Hand looms are an important craft product and comprise the largest cottage industry in the country. Millions of looms across the country are engaged in weaving cottons, silks, woolens, and other natural fibers. Each region of India specializes in a particular kind of textile craft. The whole process, from weaving to dyeing and printing, is carried out manually by family members. Young people, generation after generation, watch and learn from their elders as a matter of daily routine. Despite their specialist skills, textile workers earn very modest wages. However, because of the beauty of the art they produce, weavers, dyers, and printers will always hold an honored place in the world history of the textile arts.

PAGE 74 A group of women wearing *bandhani odhinis* (tie-dye veils) known as *pila*, a traditional gift given by parents to their daughter upon the birth of a son, in the desert region of Jaisalmer, Rajasthan.

PAGE 75 Detail of a bandhani odhini in vibrant red (traditionally worn at weddings), embellished with mirrors to produce a glittering effect in the sunlight.

OPPOSITE LEFT TOP Detail of a textile embroidered with sequins and real gold and silver thread, a technique known as *zardozi.*

OPPOSITE LEFT CENTER Detail of an embroidered Rajasthani skirt.

OPPOSITE LEFT BOTTOM Detail of an emerald green skirt embroidered with sequins and gold and silver thread, made to resemble zardozi.

OPPOSITE TOP, MIDDLE, AND BOTTOM RIGHT It is said that when Buddha attained nirvana his body was wrapped in a fabric from Varanasi (also called Benares), from which shot rays of dazzling blue, red, and yellow; indeed, Varanasi has a long history of weaving brocades for Tibetan Buddhist monasteries. Depicted here is an array of intricately patterned and colorful Tibetan *gyasar* (silk fabric with gold thread in Tibetan motifs) brocades woven in Varanasi.

ABOVE Young textile workers snip off excess threads in a weaving workshop in Varanasi, one of the many stages in the production of a brocade fabric.

ABOVE Screen-printed fabric dries in a shed in Sanganer, Rajasthan, as the sunlight gently pierces the woven cane ceiling. Sanganer is located beside the Saraswati River, whose flowing water and sandy banks radiate sunlight, drying the fabric and bringing their glowing colors to life.

OPPOSITE TOP LEFT Cotton fabric in Sanganer is draped on wooden bars to dry while a camel waits to transport it to the printer, where it will be screen or block printed.

OPPOSITE TOP RIGHT Lengths of cotton dyed green, orange, and mustard dry in the sun, one part of the dye "fixing" process. The fabric is steamed in boilers, washed thoroughly, and hung on wooden bars to dry.

OPPOSITE BOTTOM Reams of dyed cotton fabric that have been dried and ironed are piled on to a camel cart for delivery to the printer.

OPPOSITE A field of color—tie-dyed fabrics dry in the sun by the banks of the Saraswati River, in Sanganer, Rajasthan.

RIGHT Textile workers in Sanganer wash dyed fabrics by stamping on them with their bare feet.

BELOW Lengths of dyed fabrics dry in the sun in Sanganer.

ABOVE Intricately carved wood blocks are used for printing designs onto textiles.

OPPOSITE TOP LEFT Jamnabai prints a cotton fabric with vegetable dyes in Sanganer. The art of block printing can be traced back to the twelfth century. The printing process remains mostly the same, requiring limited water, space, and power. Mineral and vegetable dyes minimize pollution, making it an eco-friendly process. Today, however, the natural dyes are being replaced with faster-working chemical ones, and block printing now competes with newer, quicker screen-printing techniques.

OPPOSITE BOTTOM LEFT In Sanganer, Nasimbhai carefully chisels a wood block after the design has been traced on to it. Each block has a wooden handle, and two or three cylindrical holes are drilled into the block to facilitate air passage and the release of excess printing dye paste.

OPPOSITE TOP RIGHT A carved wood printing block, known as a *bunta*, is covered in yellow vegetable dye and is ready to be placed on to fabric. In the nineteenth and early twentieth centuries, the blocks were made of teak and soaked in oil for up to fifteen days to soften the wood. Today they are made mainly of sheeshum, a softer, lighter wood.

OPPOSITE BOTTOM RIGHT Shown here are a variety of hand-carved bunta, with designs ranging from simple to elaborate.

ETERNAL SARI

The sari, the world's oldest surviving and thriving garment, is the traditional garment worn by many women in the Indian subcontinent. The six yards of fabric in a sari are a celebration of life, skills, textures, weaves, colors, and embellishments that stretch back as far as three thousand years; the walls of the Ajanta caves depict beautiful women in arrow ikat (a special weaving technique) saris, which are still woven in that region. In the epic Sanskrit poem the *Mahabharata*, said to have been compiled in the first century B.C., Draupadi, the beautiful wife of the Pandavas, is lost to the Kauravas in a gambling duel. Draupadi prays to Krishna for help when her captors, seeking to humiliate her, pull at her sari, trying to unravel it. The sari unravels endlessly, puzzling her captors and confirming that her prayers have been answered.

Some of the great sari centers include Benares (now known by its ancient name, Varanasi), by the River Ganges; Chanderi, in Madhya Pradesh; and Kanjivaram, in South India. Over the centuries, each region has developed its own distinctive sari style, with unique fabrics, weaving techniques, motifs, and mode of draping.

In the most common draping style, the sari is wrapped around the waist, tucked into a *ghaghra* (petticoat), and pleated at the navel with one end draped over the shoulder. This end, known as the *pallu* or *pallav*, is one of the most visible sections of the sari and is woven or printed in an elaborate design, since it is the showpiece of the garment. The sari is worn over a low-cut, short-sleeved, midriff-baring blouse known as a *choli*. Not immune to the glamour of the fashion world, saris are even being created in high style: in Mumbai (formerly known as Bombay), the trendiest catwalks show off designer saris worn by glamorous models, while urban fashionistas vie for the newest fabrics, colors, and designs.

Despite regional styles and modern design influences, the sari remains timeless. Just six yards of unstitched cloth, it is one of the most feminine, fashionable, and graceful garments in the world.

PAGE 84 Many are the shades of pink in Benarasi brocade silk saris: *falsa* (dark pink berry), *rani rang* (color of queens), and *piazi* (onion pink). Brocade saris go through an elaborate process and pass through the hands of at least five artisans before they are ready to be worn. A brocade sari is the result of the combined efforts of the *kalakar* (the person who draws the pattern), the *naqshabund* (who makes the thread cards for the loom), and the *karigar* (weaver).

PAGE 85 Nandita wears a traditional Benares Katan silk sari, with a design of parrots woven on to the border, in *sidha pallu* (straight over the shoulder) style.

LEFT Skilled artisans carefully stretch dyed threads in Varanasi.

OPPOSITE BOTTOM LEFT A textile worker dyes silk in the weaving district of Varanasi.

OPPOSITE BOTTOM RIGHT A textile worker in Varanasi carries punched cards that will be used to make patterns in weaving with a Jacquard loom.

RIGHT To keep the fibers moist, a skilled weaver in Varanasi uses his mouth to spray water on the thousands of threads carefully tied to a hand loom.

BELOW A Varanasi weaver prepares his hand loom, making sure all thirty-five hundred warp threads are in the right place.

OPPOSITE TOP Floral and architectural motifs, figures, animals, and birds rendered in detailed multicolor threadwork lend the saris their elegance and vibrancy. This sari is in the Baluchari style, which originated in Bengal, and is made of deep blue-green woven silk with a colored design of *buti* (small flowers).

OPPOSITE BOTTOM An array of different sari weaves, including a typical ikat from Orissa (foreground). Ikat patterns are created when both the warp and weft threads are tie-dyed and then woven.

ABOVE Benarasi brocade saris with *zardozi* borders, which are embroidered in gold and silver threads in traditional scrolling floral designs.

RIGHT Color samples for dyeing silks.

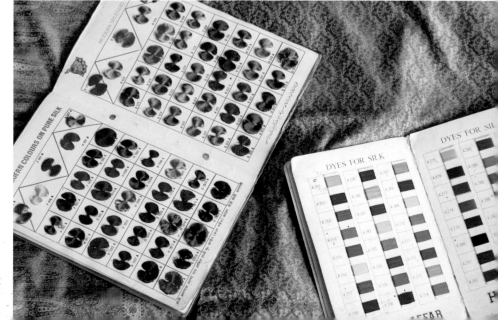

TURBANS

The English word turban derives from the Turkish *tülbend*, but this distinctive men's head covering has many other names: *pencha*, *dastar*, *sela*, *safa*, *ushnisha*, *kirita*, *patta*, *vestana*, *vestanapatta*, and *sirovestana*, to name a few. The term *pagri* is commonly used today.

Headdresses and wraps have graced men's heads in India for many centuries. As time passed, wearing a pagri became imbued with social meaning. In medieval times the pagri was regarded as a sign of honor—a symbol of dignity, respect, and authority; no one was allowed to enter the royal court without a pagri. Similarly, laying down one's pagri signified the wearer's absolute submission to another. In Rajasthan, exchanging turbans signified friendship. Trampling a pagri was considered a grave insult. Today, the pagri still retains much of its social significance; the manner of tying, coloring, and styling indicates the wearer's caste, the region he hails from, and his profession. However, unlike its Sikh counterpart, the Rajasthani pagri has no religious role.

It is said that the patterns and colors of men's turbans change every ten miles in Rajasthan. They also change according to the season. It has been estimated that there are approximately a thousand different styles and types of turbans in Rajasthan alone.

A pagri is usually eighty-two feet long and eight inches wide. A variation on the pagri, the safa, is shorter and broader, about thirty feet long and four feet wide. The pagri's size and shape are influenced by regional climate conditions. Turbans in the hot desert areas are large and loose, and farmers and shepherds, who need constant protection from the elements, wear some of the most voluminous and brightly colored turbans. Turbans also have many practical functions. A traveler might use his pagri as a pillow, a blanket, or a towel. Muddy water can be strained through the cloth of a pagri. Unraveled, it can be used in an emergency to tie to a bucket for drawing water from a well.

In addition to the garment's practical uses, the wearing of a pagri is governed by etiquette. If one is wearing a close-collared Jodhpuri coat, the tail of one's Jodhpuri pagri should reach down to the waist. If one is wearing an *achkan* (a coat that reaches the knees), the tail should extend below the hem of the coat.

PAGES 90 AND 91 Like most clothing, pagris evolved as a way of protecting the head from the elements, whether the heat of the sun, desert sandstorms, or the biting cold of winter. Soon the pagri became a form of adornment.

PAGES 92 AND 93 Shown here are just a few of the hundreds of popular styles and colors of turbans. For example, during the harvesting months of February and March, men in Rajasthan wear *falguniya* (white turbans with the ends dyed red). During the monsoon season, green and pink or yellow and red *lahariya* patterns (tie-dyed with waves or chevrons) are worn. Black *chunari* (tie-dyed with red borders) are worn for Diwali (the festival of light); saffron is worn for Dussehra (the day of Saraswati, the goddess of knowledge and learning), *mothara* (checked patterns) for Raksha Bandhan (brother's day), yellow during Basant Panchami (fifth day of spring), and *motiya* (pearl pink) during Kartika Poornima (night of the full moon in November). The *panchrangi* pagri is dyed in five different colors and is worn for festivals and special formal occasions. Other colors signify family circumstances; for instance, the dotted chunari pattern signifies a marriage or the birth of a child, while white, dark blue, or maroon may be worn for funerals.

OPPOSITE AND LEFT A young boy ties his turban while sitting on a camel in front of the Taj Mahal, in Agra.

ABOVE A man from the Bhopa community ties a turban around his son's head at the Mehrangarh Fort, Jodhpur, Rajasthan.

PUPPETS & TOYS

Since prehistoric times, people have used wood, stone, clay, and cloth to re-create figures and events from the tangible world as well as from the imaginary realm of folklore, legends, and myths. The earliest known dolls, unearthed from the site of the Indus River Valley civilization, date back more than five thousand years. In modern times, the culture of doll and toy making continues to flourish in India. Each region has its own distinct style of making fanciful playthings—which are often carved, polished, lacquered, and painted—and each toy has its own story to tell. The list of toys characteristic of rural India is endless, including whistles, trains, carts, catapults, animals, birds, fish, insects, human figures, marbles, kites, and swings.

Many recycled and natural materials, such as wood and clay, are used in the making of toys. Old clothes and fabrics are used to make stuffed animals and puppets. Empty thread spindles become the wheels of a pull cart. Other materials used to make toys include newspaper, jute and coir, string, stones, wire, and empty film cartridges.

The Rajasthani tradition of making string puppets, or *kaathputlis*, dates back more than a thousand years. The puppets are much more than decorative playthings. They are part of the traditional art of puppetry, retelling events from history, myths, folklore, and legends, accompanied by music. The stories enacted by these charming puppets often include the oral histories of various regions. Traditional puppeteers come from the nomadic community of the Bhats, moving from village to village with their boxes of kaathputlis and their musical instruments. The puppeteers and musicians usually spring from one family, having received training in their art from the older generations, who in turn learned it from their elders. No village fair, religious festival, or social gathering would be complete without a puppet show.

PAGE 96 An array of painted and colorfully clothed kaathputlis bring cheer to a bazaar in Jaipur, Rajasthan.

PAGE 97 A meticulously carved and brightly painted wooden scene—made by artisans in Andhra Pradesh, a state famous for its wood-crafting traditions—retells one of the Hindu creation myths. From the navel of Vishnu (the Preserver) grows a magnificent lotus flower. In the middle of the blossom sits Brahma (the Creator).

ABOVE Toys outside a shop in Udaipur, Rajasthan.

OPPOSITE TOP LEFT A puppet show is being performed by a skilled puppeteer and drummer. An exciting dialogue goes on between the two, providing a playful running commentary on the show. Each puppet is manipulated by strings, which are looped into the puppeteer's fingers. The other puppets lie inert on the stage until their cue, coming to life when the strings are pulled and the drums begin to beat.

OPPOSITE TOP RIGHT A young man sews bright-colored clothes for a puppet, reusing patches of old cloth, in a toy shop in Udaipur, Rajasthan.

OPPOSITE BOTTOM Characters from the Rajasthani puppet repertoire are displayed outside a toy shop in Udaipur, Rajasthan.

OPPOSITE TOP Brightly painted, carved wood figures represent Issar and Gauri, Rajasthani folk interpretations of Shiva and Parvati, who symbolize the perfect couple. Ganesh, Remover of Obstacles, stands by.

OPPOSITE BOTTOM Wooden horses, figures, and puppets are set out in a bazaar in Udaipur, Rajasthan. Toys are used in the celebration of festivals to help children understand their cultural traditions and customs.

ABOVE A group of carved and painted wooden figures depict a charming band of women musicians in Udaipur, Rajasthan.

RIGHT Painted wooden horses.

chapter
12

CERAMICS

The concept of a clay vessel made by hand and turned on a wheel is intimately connected to the creation story of nearly every ancient civilization. Lord Brahma, the creator of the vast pantheon of Indian gods and goddesses, was said to have made the figure of the first man out of clay and, with his own breath, to have brought life into the world. Through the art of pottery, modern India manages to remain in touch with its deepest cultural and artistic traditions.

More than a million potters across the country make utilitarian and decorative objects and vessels of great beauty in a variety of decorative techniques—techniques that have not changed despite the passing of time. The ubiquity and functionality of ceramic vessels also remain the same. Indian tea is served to long-distance-rail passengers in small, biodegradable clay cups that can be thrown away after using. Village women gather at the local well in the late afternoon to gossip and chat before filling large clay pots with water, which they balance gracefully on their heads and carry back to their homes. The fired clay filters and purifies the water, keeping it cool during hot summer months. Even in the cities, where modern refrigeration has become common, people continue to use the clay pots because they like the taste they impart to beverages.

Pottery-making techniques from other cultures had their own influence on the Indian forms of this art. Finely glazed Chinese porcelain first began to appear in India in the early fourteenth century. The refined techniques used to make Persian pottery, with its intricate painted pattern and iridescent glazes, were brought in by the Mughal people two centuries later. This tradition has continued to thrive in Jaipur, where the famous "blue pottery," with its distinctive blue, white, and yellow tones and flower-and-bird motifs, is sold both locally and around the world.

One of the most lively pottery bazaars in India is located inside Jaipur near the Tripoliya Gate, where thousands of fired and painted pottery vessels are piled high, waiting for customers. The work is brought in from villages outside of Jaipur, and some of it may be painted and finished while you wait. Bright-hued clay toys, lamps, flower pots, pen stands, and wall plaques made for festivals and domestic use are all on display. Business is brisk on the sidewalk of this most colorful Indian town.

PAGE 102 Rajasthani women, dressed in their finest, carry clay water pots on their heads during a marriage procession. Because water symbolizes an auspicious and fertile beginning for the young couple, the pots make appropriate and welcome gifts for the bride and groom.

PAGE 103 Hand-thrown clay water pots painted with a striking band of gold are sold in the Jaipur market and used for keeping water clean and cool during the long summer months.

OPPOSITE AND THIS PAGE This lively pottery bazaar in central Jaipur is filled with everything from ritual lamps to children's toys. The pieces are handmade or thrown on a potter's wheel in villages on the outskirts of Jaipur, where they are also fired in traditional brick-lined kilns. Once they are brought to the town, women sit in the bazaar and paint the pottery in bright colors to attract buyers stocking up on ceramics for Diwali, the Hindu festival of light.

Jaipur is justly famous for its "blue pottery," which can be purchased in shops all over the city. The high-fired clay vessels are painted and glazed with floral and animal designs in traditional shades of blue, yellow, and white (although some new motifs and colors have recently emerged).

OPPOSITE LEFT A local goat wanders by a display of glazed vessels and tiles arranged in the courtyard of the village workshop.

LEFT A striking blue pottery vase, waiting to be packed and sent to the local market, stands alone on an azure wall.

ABOVE Small vases, containers, and toothbrush holders are painted and glazed in shades of blue and white, the colors favored by the Jaipur potters.

JEWELS & BANGLES

Jewelry making has been an unbroken tradition for over five thousand years. Examples of exquisite jewelry can be found carved on the sculptures of Ellora, which date back to 2000 B.C. The craft of jewelry making has been given royal patronage since ancient times, when maharajas competed with each other to possess the most exquisite and magnificent pieces of jewelry. Today, jewelry wearers are not limited to royalty or even humans. Ornaments are crafted for *murtis* (sculptures of gods) and animals, especially elephants, horses, camels, and cows.

Indian jewelry ranges from religious to purely aesthetic, and styles vary from one region to another. In the villages of Rajasthan, women wear silver—heavy, intricately engraved chunks of it around the neck, ankles, and wrists; lighter chain belts around the waist; dangling earrings; nose rings; toe rings; and more. Each piece has a particular name and importance.

Jaipur is located in a rich mineral belt of marble and precious and semiprecious stones, making it a bountiful marketplace for extraordinary jewels. Emerald, garnet, agate, amethyst, topaz, and lapis lazuli are all found locally. Each piece of jewelry is the product of a long chain of skilled artisans: the *nyarriya* refines the gold, the *sangsaz* polishes and cuts the stones, the *manihar* prepares the enamel, the *sonar* makes the bezels for setting the stones and fashions the jewel using patterned molds, the *chattera* engraves the ground, the *meenakar* enamels and fires it, and the *kundansaz* sets the stone in a mixture of lacquer and antimony and, when it has solidified, cold-sets it with hammered gold wire. The sonar polishes and cleans the piece and the *patwari* puts the finishing touch of twisted gold and silver cord, with its tasseled pendant and beaded knot—twisting the threads between his big toe, knee and index finger—in a flashing intricate cat's-cradle.

The names and varieties of bangles are seemingly endless. *Kangana*, *valaya*, *kada*, *gajulu*, *chooda*, *choodi*, *karha*, and *bangri* are some of the names, and the many materials from which they are made include glass, plastic, metal, conch shell, and ivory. Some are even lacquered. Everywhere you go, you see girls wearing bangles around both wrists, since it is considered inauspicious to have bare arms. Every town in India has a bangle bazaar; rows of crowded shops are filled with women and girls buying new bangles—filigreed, carved, gem-encrusted, enameled, or made of colored glass.

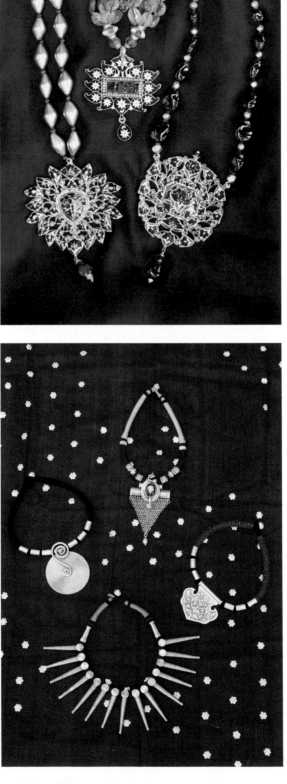

PAGE 108 A Rajasthani woman in her sparkling finery wears a *nath* (nose ring), attached with a chain to a *karanphool jhoomka* (literally "the flower of the ear"). Around her neck she is wearing necklaces, charms, and amulets and a *hussli* (a collar of coiled thick silver wire, larger in the middle and tapering toward the ends). An ornamented silver armlet adorns her forearm.

PAGE 109 These ingots of pure silver will one day be transformed into gleaming jewelry.

OPPOSITE TOP LEFT Contemporary necklaces in the *kundan* style (the Mughal-inspired art of setting stones in gold) with polished emeralds, uncut diamonds, rubies, and gold beads. In the kundan technique, gold is reduced to a pure state so that it is malleable and can bond without heat, allowing the luminous colors of emeralds, rubies, pearls, and other precious stones to show their intense clarity. Gems are embedded in gold rather than secured by a rim or claw.

OPPOSITE TOP RIGHT The reverse sides of the same pendants have been ornamented in *meenakari* (enamelwork) to protect the gold, which in its pure state is so soft that it can easily wear away. *Ab-e-leher* (waves of water), *tote-ka-par* (parrot's wing), green, and *khoon-e-kabootar* (pigeon's blood), a highly prized deep, translucent red, are some of the names given to enamel colors.

OPPOSITE BOTTOM An array of contemporary necklaces strung with gold ornaments and beads, inspired by traditional folk and classical designs.

ABOVE Traditional silver armlets, bangles, and a *hussli* worn by women in rural Rajasthan.

LEFT Sparkling temptations. Every girl in India, rich or poor, possesses dozens of colored bangles to match her clothes. Women and girls buy them for every festival, every celebration, and every occasion. As you pass bangle shops you can watch bangle sellers expertly massaging women's hands, pushing rings upon rings of colored glass bangles on to their arms. It is said that young men secretly envy bangle sellers, who have the opportunity to hold the delicate wrists of women as they try on bangles.

OPPOSITE TOP On Bagru Street, Jaipur, Zarina Begum, a bangle maker, ornaments a lacquered bangle with rhinestones, which are heated so that they will adhere to the lacquer.

OPPOSITE BOTTOM LEFT A Rajasthani woman wears colored bangles that exactly match the hues in her *odhini* (veil).

OPPOSITE BOTTOM RIGHT A young boy following in his family's traditional occupation makes a lacquered bangle at Kuchaman Fort, Rajasthan.

LEFT AND OPPOSITE BOTTOM RIGHT
The Ahirs of Rajasthan and the Rabaris of Gujarat, pastoral tribes, cover their entire arms with broad, plain white bangles made of camel bone or, more recently, plastic. Unmarried girls wear them from the wrist to the elbow, and married women wear them from the elbow upward as far as the underarm. Nomadic tribes wear their savings in the form of jewelry, so that if a calamity such as a drought or famine strikes, they can simply go to the closest town to sell their portable assets.

OPPOSITE TOP AND BOTTOM LEFT
Young dancers from various Rajasthani pastoral tribes are decked out in their finest jewelry at the Pushkar Camel Fair.

OPPOSITE AND THIS PAGE Young women sport dazzling color, texture, and fabric combinations with their traditional jewelry, along with some modern additions: colored hairpins.

MUSIC & DANCE

Music and dance are an integral part of life in India and remain important sources of religious inspiration, cultural expression, and pure entertainment. Styles include multiple varieties of popular, classical, and folk music, the latter being mostly composed for dancing. Indian folk music reflects the rich folklore, heroic ballads, fables, and lives of people in rural India.

The shimmering sands and contoured desolation of the Thar desert of Rajasthan have cradled the ancient folk traditions of this region for centuries. The activities of daily life and the legends of heroism and romance are all captured in the region's vibrant and spirited music and dance. The infinite variations of folk music and dance punctuate the desert, turning the barren, harsh land into a lively basin of color, creativity, and rhythm.

One of the most popular stories sung in Rajasthan takes the form of musical theater and celebrates the adventures of Pabuji Ramdeo, fourteenth-century hero and member of the Bhopas (a community of wandering balladeers, considered priest-singers, who sing the stories of folk deities). Accompanied by a *ravanhatta* (stringed instrument played with a bow), the ballads of the *Pabuji ka Phad* (the Scroll of Pabuji) are sung by a Bhopa and a Bhopi (his veiled wife) in front of a *phad*, a painted scroll, which functions as a portable temple. Vignettes of Pabuji's life are portrayed in comic-strip fashion on the scroll. Entire village communities gather to view the evening performances. As the two performers sing the ballad in full-throated voices accompanied by the ravanhatta, the Bhopi lifts an oil lantern to illuminate the particular portion of the scroll where these deeds have been painted.

The rhythm of India lies in its folk music and dance. It is the music of the people and of the thousands of villages that dot the country. Music and dance have developed into a rich, multilayered, vibrant, and creative art form that influences not only mainstream Indian music but also much of today's world music.

PAGE 118 Musicians are ready to entertain at the Pushkar Camel Fair, Rajasthan.

PAGE 119 The Indian harmonium evolved from the accordion, a European import, but it has developed into a bicultural instrument. It is also known as a *peti* (suitcase), since it bears a resemblance to a suitcase or trunk. The keyboard is European but it has a number of drone reeds that are particularly Indian. The harmonium shown here is at the Jaipur music bazaar.

LEFT A Rajasthani nose-flute player demonstrates his instrument in Jaipur.

OPPOSITE TOP LEFT AND CENTER Musician-singers from the Bhopa community of priest-singers play the ravanhatta in Rajasthan.

OPPOSITE TOP RIGHT A Rajasthani musician demonstrates the *bansuri* (bamboo flute).

OPPOSITE BOTTOM LEFT A *sadhu* (nomadic ascetic) musician poses outside Jaipur, Rajasthan, with his instrument, a reed instrument with an air reservoir in an animal-skin bag, similar to a bagpipe.

OPPOSITE BOTTOM CENTER A musician plays a *surinda*, a small precursor of the violin, in Rajasthan.

OPPOSITE BOTTOM RIGHT A musician-singer in Jaisalmer, the desert region of Rajasthan, plays an *ektaar* (single string), believed to be the oldest stringed instrument in India. The ektaar is described in ancient Sanskrit texts as the *ekatantri vina* (one-stringed lute).

ABOVE Purulia Chhau dancers decked out in dazzling costumes and headdresses get ready to perform. In the barren land of West Bengal, tribal inhabitants, multilayered influences from Vedic literature, Hinduism, and martial folklore have combined to shape the Purulia Chhau dances, which have only one message—the triumph of good over evil.

RIGHT Colorful Purulia Chhau masks from West Bengal are molded from clay and papier-mâché or carved out of wood, and elaborately painted with rich, stylized makeup. The headdresses are generally made of a variety of light materials such as shoal pith, sponge, or papier-mâché and are decorated with strands of artificial pearls and small mirrored discs.

LEFT A young Rajasthani dancer from the Kabeliya community stands dressed from head to toe in her dazzling costume and jewelry. Befitting the Kabeliya community's traditional occupation, which is to catch snakes and trade snake venom for the curing of illnesses, their dance resembles the movements of snakes. Dancers swirl in their skirts, swaying sinuously to the accompaniment of musicians.

BELOW Dancers put on their makeup as they get ready to perform various Rajasthani folk dances.

OPPOSITE TOP LEFT Rama Vaidyanathan, shown here, is a renowned Bharatnatyam classical dancer. Originating as an art of temple dancers, Bharatnatyam is a highly stylized dance form depicting the manifestation of the eternal universe through the celebration of beauty.

OPPOSITE TOP RIGHT The Chari dance is performed by young women balancing clay pots, often outfitted with lit oil lamps, on their heads. These skilled dancers are trained from early childhood, performing graceful, rigorous, and acrobatic movements as flames swirl above them. Musicians accompany the dancers with pulsating rhythms and full-throated singing voices.

OPPOSITE BOTTOM These girls are performing the Ghoomer dance, one of the most popular folk dances. A wide variety of musical instruments are used, ranging from soft tinklers to thunderous kettledrums, from rustic-looking resonators for basic rhythm to the *sarangi* for elegant and fully developed bowing and plucking.

SHEESH MAHAL
magic with mirrors and glass

Walk into a grand mansion or palace in India and you will likely be greeted by thousands of glittering pieces of faceted mirror and colored glass, set in intricate gilded plaster patterns. The popular story behind the origin of this labor-intensive technique comes from a nineteenth-century maharaja who ordered a shipload of Venetian mirrors, meant to be installed in his newly completed palace. Unfortunately, the mirrors arrived broken, shattered into tiny pieces and jagged shards. Undeterred, the local artisans cut the remains into round and geometric shapes and  set them into the walls of the palace, creating a brilliant glittering effect when lit by oil lamps and candles. However, the technique of mirror work goes back much further and may have originated in Persia, where it appears on the walls of palaces built as early as the fifteenth century, and then arrived in India with the Mughals a hundred years later.

The Rajput rulers of Rajasthan and the Mughal emperors both used this technique in their palaces, and mirror work is even found inside the imperial baths. In the arid areas of western India, where some of the finest mirror work is found, mirrored walls create the effect of water sparkling in a desert oasis, or a starry night sky. Some special palace apartments, like the Sheesh Mahal at Kuchaman and the Anup Mahal at Junagadh Fort in Bikaner, have now assumed the status of major works of art in their own right.

Two major traditional centers of mirror- and glass-making were Kapadwanj in Gujarat and Firozabad in Uttar Pradesh. Glass was laid down in thin sheets and the backs were coated with mercury. Blown-glass mirrored spheres were also made, some as large as eight inches in diameter. They were then broken into small, concave pieces that, when set into the wall, reflected light, shadow, and images around the room.

Today these workshops make reproductions of antique chandeliers and cut-glass furniture for the Indian and Western markets. But, as everything old becomes new again, mirror work is returning to popularity. Builders of private homes are now incorporating touches of glittering mirror work in their design concepts. Owners of luxury heritage hotels have begun commissioning master artisans to embellish the walls of their old forts and palaces using mostly traditional geometric and floral patterns. Fortunately, this precious art is alive and well.

PAGE 126 The walls of the Sheesh Mahal inside the palace apartments at the very top of Kuchaman Fort are completely covered with faceted pieces of mirror set in frames of gilded plaster. No expense was spared in the decoration of this opulent and glittering room, considered to contain some of the finest mirror work in Rajasthan.

PAGE 127 A scene of a mythical city is depicted on the walls of the Kuchaman Sheesh Mahal using a traditional technique of painting on glass and carved and gilded plasterwork.

PAGE 128 The walls and ceiling of the nineteenth-century Maharaja Suite at the Samode Haveli in Jaipur sparkle with thousands of faceted pieces of handcrafted mirror. Locally made block-printed bedspreads made cover the carved wooden beds. The entrance to the suite retains the original frescoes painted with floral motifs.

PAGE 129 TOP Deep within the inner precincts of the Junagadh Fort, the Anup Mahal was created as a ceremonial throne room by Maharaja Anup Singh, one of the greatest rulers of the desert kingdom of Bikaner. The refined opulence of this jewel-like seventeenth-century apartment ranks with the finest anywhere in the country. The superb walls are adorned with floral arabesques executed in a traditional technique using carved and gilded plaster set with faceted mirror and colored glass.

PAGE 129 CENTER The principal reception hall of the Alsisar Haveli in Jaipur has recently been restored to its original splendor by master artisans. Set with thousands of pieces of faceted mirror, the grand curving arch spans the entire hall.

PAGE 129 BOTTOM The sitting room at Alsisar Haveli is an elegant room for socializing. Floral motifs painted by local artisans flank mirrored arches. Through this doorway, visitors glimpse vivid stained-glass windows.

THIS PAGE AND OPPOSITE The delightful Khimsar Desert Resort is set in the middle of a vast crater formed by natural sand dunes. The walls of the five cottages have been constructed out of plastered mud, and the rooms decorated by traditional village artists. Sparkling like the Milky Way at night, the bedroom ceilings and walls of each cottage are set with countless small circular and diamond-shaped mirror pieces. Desert plants and even a camel being led by a bejeweled maiden through the dunes become mirrored works of art.

FIT FOR A KING
gold and glitter

Occasionally, in the history of architecture, a great patron with a grand vision appears, endowed with extraordinary taste and the necessary resources and commitment to complete the project. Maharaja Anup Singh, the seventeenth-century ruler of the desert kingdom of Bikaner, was such a man.

Anup Singh served as a general in the Mughal army and spent much of his life fighting battles far away from home. He led the decisive assault on the Deccani fortress of Golconda in the south of India, the home of the fabled Koh-i-Noor diamond, in 1687. Weary from decades of fighting, he returned to Bikaner, where he commissioned the creation of the Anup Mahal, a sumptuous and regal hall set deep inside the great Junagadh Fort, where he had been born.

Only the most trusted ministers, worthy courtiers, and important foreign delegations were received in this important room, and it was imperative that the decor have a grandeur and beauty befitting the power and status of the maharaja. His master artisans, executing his vision of a grand and sumptuous room, did not disappoint. Anup Singh sat within a raised alcove on a golden platform covered with brocade cushions embroidered with pure gold thread. The curving arch above his head and the surrounding walls were set with thousands of tiny faceted pieces of glittering mirror and colored and foiled glass set in raised borders of gilded plaster. It must have been like sitting inside a jewel box studded with emeralds, rubies, and diamonds.

Magnificent Persian and Mughal carpets covered the floor in front, where the courtiers sat looking up at the ruler. Master artists drew the outlines of scrolling floral arabesques and geometric patterns on the walls, columns, and ceiling. The painting was executed with a pigment created from ground semiprecious stone mixed with gum arabic, and gold leaf details were added at the end to enhance the overall splendor. At each end of the apartment, exquisite carved wooden doors, painted and lacquered with floral patterns, were added, leading to adjoining rooms.

Beautifully preserved with a minimum of restoration, the Anup Mahal, after more than two centuries, continues to express the aesthetic vision of a great king and the exquisite skills of the nameless master artisans who made it all possible.

SRI PRATAP NIWAS

PAGE 132 The sumptuous Anup Mahal, inside Bikaner's Junagadh Fort, epitomizes the extravagant and exotic splendor of royal India. Built by Maharaja Anup Singh at the end of the seventeenth century as a hall of private audience, every inch of the walls and ceiling was embellished using the finest and richest craftsmanship available. The maharaja is believed to have sat on a golden throne set with jewels. Thousands of pieces of glittering cut mirror and foil-backed glass have been set into the curving arch above. The ceiling is a masterpiece of carved and gilded wood.

PAGE 133 Detail of a delicately carved and gilded column from the Anup Mahal. The fine lacquer painting has been burnished by rubbing with small pieces of agate, which creates a jewel-like sheen.

OPPOSITE This antique *hindola*, a ritual swing on which the image or painting of a god is placed, stands inside one of the many exquisitely appointed apartments within the Anup Mahal complex.

ABOVE Due to the dry climate of Bikaner, very little restoration has been needed inside the royal apartments of the Junagadh Fort. These beautifully painted doors retain their vibrant colors even after hundreds of years. The walls are painted and gilded with intricate floral patterns and trays and platters of fruit and sweetmeats, which evoke the splendor of the royal celebrations and banquets that took place in these magnificent rooms.

LEFT Carved stone screens set with colored glass illuminate this unrestored wall inside the Chandra Mahal, or Moon Palace, at the Junagadh Fort.

OPPOSITE The walls of the striking Badal Mahal, or Chamber of Clouds, inside the Junagadh Fort, are painted with monsoon clouds, lightning, and rain showers, showing the importance of rain in this desert kingdom.

LEFT Narrow corridors connect a series of royal chambers inside the fort. Light streams in through carved *jali* screens set with multicolored pieces of cut glass.

ABOVE A masterpiece of painted lacquer work, this original door stands, in unrestored splendor, at one end of the Anup Mahal. Persian carpets adorn the floor, and the ceiling is carved and gilded with interlocking geometric patterns.

PAINTING & MURALS

The *Kama Sutra*, an ancient, arcane treatise most celebrated for its erotic passages, described painting as one of the sixty-four arts that an elegant gentleman or lady needed to master in order to be truly cultivated. On a more basic level, the need to tell a story and record events through pictures is an integral aspect of human life. The walls of one's dwelling make a handy canvas. So, naturally, painting and depicting stories of life and legend on the walls of a cave, village hut, or palace have been part of humans' basic artistic expression for hundreds of thousands of years.

In another method of illustrating stories, the Patua storytellers of Bengal paint long paper scrolls with tales of epic adventures or contemporary life. Wandering from village to village, these itinerant performers narrate their stories in a lively performance of dance and song, slowly unrolling their scrolls as the events unfold. Wall paintings in Rajasthan serve much the same purpose—preserving, recording, and narrating the heroic legends and exploits of gods and goddesses, maharajas, and even star-crossed lovers escaping across the desert dunes. Some of the most beautiful and spectacular wall paintings are found in the many forts and palaces that have, in recent years, been converted into luxury heritage hotels. Because they were applied to wet plaster, the elaborate paintings have faded very little with the passage of time and retained the original vivid colors, which were obtained by crushing and grinding a variety of semiprecious stones, minerals, and plants.

The Samode Palace, located about an hour's drive north of Jaipur, contains some of the most vibrant and colorful wall paintings in India. Gulabchand Karigar, a gifted artist whose family has been living in Samode for generations, worked for the last forty years on the brilliant restoration of the wall paintings inside the palace, under the supervision and patronage of the Samode royal family. Although he is now retired, he clearly remembers how he and his team of skilled apprentices carefully cleaned the walls, ground and mixed the colors, and meticulously restored the delicate flowers, trees, and scenes of courtly life that adorn the walls of this magnificent palace.

PAGE 138 The vibrant colors and charming scenes of courtly life painted on the walls of the Samode Palace conjure images of a world of regal splendor that has all but disappeared. In this panel from the private apartments of the ruler, pairs of lovely maidens relax in a delightful garden inhabited by strutting peacocks, green parrots, and a host of other exotic birds.

PAGE 139 During the day, the Sultan Mahal (Palace of the King) at the Samode Palace in Rajasthan is bathed in glowing sunlight. The walls, arches, and alcoves are covered with floral frescoes and paintings.

FAR LEFT Examples of the superb architectural detailing found in the Jodhpur Mehrangarh Fort, these sculptured half columns set into the wall are painted with tones of blue, green, and terracotta, a color combination found in many palaces in western Rajasthan.

OPPOSITE TOP RIGHT Some of the liveliest narrative wall paintings in Rajasthan are found inside the Mehrangarh Fort. Here, gallant Rajput warriors gallop across the desert in hot pursuit of wild boar and deer.

OPPOSITE CENTER LEFT Painted on the outer walls of the Deogarh Palace, this life-size prancing horse, adorned with a complete set of richly decorated trappings, welcomes guests as they enter the fort.

OPPOSITE CENTER RIGHT Stormy monsoon clouds and flashes of lightning cover the walls of the Badal Mahal, or Chamber of Clouds, inside the Junagadh Fort in Bikaner. Nearly hidden inside a recessed niche, Lord Krishna and his consort, Radha, stand on a golden dais in the middle of a flower garden.

OPPOSITE BOTTOM Extensive renovation of heritage properties across Rajasthan has given new work to teams of traditional artists. This elaborately painted ceiling inside the principal reception hall at the Kuchaman Fort draws its inspiration from the past while allowing the master artist who designed it to express his individual creativity. A delightful detail from the same ceiling portrays a Rajput princess amusing herself with a pet bird.

TOP LEFT Detail of an elaborately gilded and painted ceiling inside the private palace apartments at the Kuchaman Fort in central Rajasthan.

TOP RIGHT The image of Lord Ganesh is considered highly auspicious and appears above the entrance doorway and on the walls of many homes, forts, palaces, and temples. This beautifully painted wall panel from the Kuchaman Fort portrays the god in a particularly luxurious manner, covered in jewels and wearing a golden crown.

BOTTOM LEFT This procession of ladies-in-waiting from the Sunehri Mahal, or Chamber of Gold, inside the upper Kuchaman Fort reveals the complex mix of artistic styles in fashion during the seventeenth century. Their eyes are Persian, their costumes are Rajput, and their royal regalia come straight out of the Mughal court.

BOTTOM RIGHT Floating on a lotus leaf, Lord Krishna serenades his adoring Radha with the divine music of his flute. The walls of the Samode Haveli in Jaipur are among the most richly decorated in the city.

THIS PAGE The Patuas, a traditional community of singer-artists from Bengal in eastern India, paint long paper and cloth scrolls in a vivid comic-strip style to illustrate cultural, social, and religious events drawn from both past and present. Slowly unrolling their colorful scrolls, these gifted performers, through a lively combination of narration, song, and dance, ensure that precious stories and folk tales will never be forgotten. The scrolls shown here, photographed at the Crafts Museum in Delhi, were painted by Jaba and Mantu Chitrakar and their daughter, Sonia. Chitrakar, their family name, means "maker of pictures."

OPPOSITE Gulabchand Karigar, a master artist from Samode, sits at his small desk, mixing his stone-ground paints and creating a series of beautiful miniatures in his unique style. He is famous throughout the state of Jaipur for restoring and recreating the wall paintings inside the Samode Palace.

OPPOSITE Constructed entirely out of mud and straw, this desert house on the road to Jaisalmer is decorated with wall paintings and a sign above the door wishing visitors a happy Diwali.

THIS PAGE Detailed decorative patterns and scenes of desert life are painted on the smooth mud walls of the Mandawa Desert Resort by local folk artists. The flat white pigment, which contrasts well with the earthy color of the walls, is made from a mixture of chalk and lime.

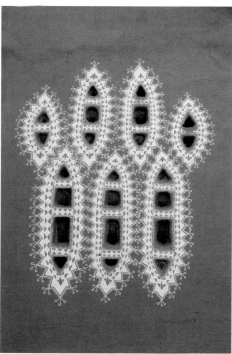

chapter 18

STONEWORK & CARVERS

India has been blessed with a rich abundance and variety of geological wealth. For centuries, Indians have put that wealth to use in magnificent fortresses, palaces, temples, and mosques—using stone as a primary building material and employing master carvers who deftly carve stone into intricate and complex patterns. Over time, the legendary quarries of India have become identified with certain historical periods and dynastic styles of architecture.

Jaisalmer, a sprawling fortified city located in the western desert of Rajasthan, was built with golden limestone quarried locally. Akbar, one of the greatest Mughal emperors, constructed his capital cities of Agra and Fatehpur Sikri out of mottled red sandstone, which became synonymous with Mughal architecture. His grandson, Shah Jahan, created the fabled Taj Mahal as an eternal memorial to his beloved Mumtaz Mahal on the bank of the Jumna River in Agra. The luminous white marble used in its construction was brought by bullock cart from Makrana in central Rajasthan, more than six hundred miles away. Delicate flowering plants, carved in deep relief and inlaid with precious stone by master artisans, adorn the walls of this remarkable monument. Three centuries later, Rabindranath Tagore would describe the Taj Mahal as "a teardrop on the cheek of time."

Agra is still the main center for *pietre dure*, or hard stone inlay. Skilled artisans continue to practice this rare traditional art. The work begins with the slicing of large blocks of semiprecious stone, such as lapis lazuli, malachite, agate, amethyst, aventurine, and mother-of-pearl, which are imported from around the world. Taking a thin slice of semiprecious stone, the artisan cuts the brittle material into traditional geometric or floral patterns. The design is then dug out of the base marble, forming the top of a decorative table or box, and the shaped pieces are set in with a strong adhesive. The entire surface is then polished until it achieves a brilliant shine. A single table can take three to four months to make, depending on the size and complexity of the design. The skill and traditional technique of Indian stone carvers and inlay artisans have not diminished with the passage of centuries as new orders and commissions continue to pour in from around the world.

PAGE 146 A master carver puts the final polish on a white marble figure of Lord Krishna inside his workshop on the Street of the Marble Workers in the heart of Jaipur. He uses a small emery stick and a selection of colored powders, which, after many hours of labor, will give a lustrous ivory-colored sheen to the marble.

PAGE 147 Agra is the traditional center for the art of semiprecious hard stone inlay, known as *pietre dure*, which was brought to India by Italian artisans who arrived during the Mughal period. Many of the skilled inlay artisans working in India can trace their origins back to the seventeenth century, when their ancestors decorated the Taj Mahal and other great Mughal palaces and monuments. This striking white marble table has been inlaid in radiating floral patterns with a variety of semiprecious stones, including malachite, lapis lazuli, turquoise, carnelian, and mother-of-pearl.

OPPOSITE TOP LEFT Similar to a puzzle in its complexity, a flower pattern is being put together with hundreds of small slices of red agate and other semiprecious stones.

OPPOSITE BOTTOM LEFT A traditional inlay artisan works on a panel created out of thousands of semiprecious stone pieces at the Frozen Music workshop in Jaipur.

OPPOSITE RIGHT Dark-blue lapis lazuli, imported from the mines of Afghanistan, is used widely in semiprecious stone inlay and in the making of exquisite jewelry.

RIGHT TOP This striking inlaid table, created out of hundreds of pieces of colored marble, echoes an early Roman mosaic floor.

RIGHT CENTER In order to appeal to a larger global market, many inlay artisans re-create Islamic, Chinese, and European designs. This still life, inspired by a seventeenth-century Florentine panel, has been inlaid on a green marble base with a variety of semiprecious stones at the Frozen Music atelier in Jaipur. Varun Seth, the guiding force behind this remarkable workshop, sources his inlay stones from around the world, and he constantly challenges his skilled artisans to stretch their artistic abilities.

RIGHT BOTTOM Designed after an original Tibetan tiger rug design, this unique inlaid table was commissioned from Frozen Music by a Russian industrialist.

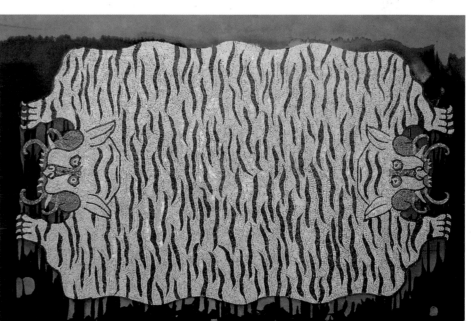

LEFT Sandstone blocks are sorted and smoothed by local village women in a workshop off the Jaipur-Agra highway. They are wearing colorful tie-dyed *odhinis* known as half-saris, which can be seen in many areas of Rajasthan.

ABOVE The complex geometric design of the ninth-century step well at Abaneri near Jaipur is truly an engineering marvel. Its design ensures that, regardless of the water level, villagers will always be able to wash their clothes and draw drinking water for their homes.

LEFT Skilled artisans depend heavily on commissioned work to survive, and orders for particular pieces help them to maintain a high standard of quality. Rajkumari Rajyashree, the princess of Bikaner, supports local arts and crafts just as her family has done for centuries. A master carver has created a beautiful white marble table, two doves, and a palm tree wall decoration for the entrance porch of her residence, recently constructed on the grounds of Lallgarh Palace, the ancestral home of the maharajas of Bikaner.

BELOW This large lotus-shaped fountain was carved from a single block of white marble at the Frozen Music workshop in Jaipur. The skilled carving recalls the fountains of Mughal India, but the interpretation is fresh and contemporary.

OPPOSITE TOP Lord Krishna and his consort, Radha, stand together in a small workshop on the Street of the Marble Workers in Jaipur.

OPPOSITE BOTTOM These monumental elephants, seemingly emerging from a stone wall, greet visitors as they enter the outer courtyard of Shiv Niwas Palace in Udaipur.

LEFT Some of the finest medieval stone carving in North India can be found on the walls of the imposing tenth-century Abaneri temple dedicated to the mother goddess, located near the stone-carving town of Sikandra on the Jaipur-Agra highway.

BELOW Gracing the building's entrance walls, this charming marble panel carved with a prancing elephant was recently commissioned by the Udaivilas Hotel in Udaipur.

RIGHT The Lallgarh Palace in Bikaner was commissioned by Maharaja Ganga Singh at the end of the nineteenth century. This remarkable carved red sandstone façade, an interior wall within the Lakshmi Vilas wing, was designed by Sir Samuel Swinton Jacob, a leading scholar and architect of the time. The intricacy and complexity of the design and the quality of the craftsmanship remain unrivaled.

BELOW The golden-limestone walls of the sixteenth-century Parsvanath Jain temple inside the Jaisalmer Fort are completely covered with carvings of mythological creatures, gods, goddesses, and celestial guardian figures.

POOLS, FOUNTAINS, & PAVILIONS OF PLEASURE

The Indian climate can be harsh and dry for months on end, until finally blessed relief in the form of monsoon rain comes in June. Suddenly, the vegetation bursts into a hundred shades of green and flowers bloom across the desert and mountain valleys. The monsoon season, which lasts for two to three months, is a romantic time when Sanskrit poets traditionally sent messages to lovers who were soon to be reunited. It is also the time that the hundreds of thousands of pools, fountains, and step wells slowly begin to fill with water, crucial for survival in the long dry season that follows.

Pools, fountains, and pavilions of pleasure are often positioned in and around large formal gardens built over the centuries by aristocratic nobles, Hindu maharajas, and Mughal emperors. As benevolent rulers, they saw it as part of their duty to provide an adequate water supply for their subjects. Through dams and other methods of water harvesting, they collected water, which would then feed the large pools, elaborate fountains, and step wells used to irrigate as well as beautify the land. For the rulers responsible for these remarkable engineering achievements, there was a further benefit: by taming the flow of water and creating magnificent gardens, the rulers clearly demonstrated their power and signaled a clear intention to remain in place.

The inspiration for the architecture and design of these beautiful structures came from many sources. Ancient and medieval historians describe the beauty of terraced gardens built inside palaces and around early Buddhist shrines. The Mughals, arriving from Central Asia in 1526, brought with them the concept of the traditional Persian *char-bagh* garden, which was divided into four quadrants filled with flowing water, fruit trees, and fragrant flowers and separated by water channels that led into a series of elegant lotus-shaped fountains.

Open pavilions covered with domed or slanting roofs were constructed inside the palace grounds and gardens and were devoted to pure pleasure. The ruler and the ladies of the court would recline on silk and velvet cushions and enjoy fireworks displays and dance and music performances in these pavilions. Today, many of these legendary forts and palaces have been converted into heritage hotels where visitors can, for a brief moment, experience life as a maharaja.

PAGE 156 Water jets spray from all sides of a large marble fountain positioned at the center of Samode Bagh, a traditional Mughal-style garden north of Jaipur.

PAGE 157 Long paved walkways cooled by lotus-bud-shaped fountains lead to an elegant arched pavilion where guests can relax and escape from the hot desert sun. Charming tents fitted with green marble bathrooms have been set up behind the pavilion in the back part of the Samode garden, where guests can stay overnight.

ABOVE The elegant turquoise-tiled pool at the Udai Kothi Hotel has a panoramic view of Lake Pichola beyond. The cusped white arches inlaid with semiprecious stone are typical of the refined palace architecture of Udaipur.

OPPOSITE TOP LEFT Sheltered by the arched stone walls of the original stables inside the Khimsar Fort, the newly constructed swimming pool offers welcome relief from the desert sun.

OPPOSITE TOP RIGHT Framed by steps laid in strict geometric patterns with black-and-white tiles, this long pool at Udaivilas in Udaipur is perfect for relaxing and swimming laps.

OPPOSITE CENTER LEFT Tucked away inside a charming garden pavilion, the swimming pool at Samode Bagh retains its original antique marble water slide, which offers guests a quick and rather quaint way to enter the pool. Mosaic tiles laid in floral arabesques decorate the bottom of the pool.

OPPOSITE CENTER RIGHT The swimming pool at the Udai Kothi Hotel in Udaipur is surrounded by domed pavilions and a wall pierced with jali screens, offering both privacy and a sense of space to guests.

OPPOSITE BOTTOM LEFT Cool and classical, the pool at Devigarh has a beautiful view of the Aravalli mountain range, which runs from one end of Rajasthan to the other.

OPPOSITE BOTTOM RIGHT A number of exquisite gardens have been created inside Udai Vilas to delight and charm visitors. The grand Solar Garden has been designed around a series of stepped water channels that terminate in a large pool, where the dramatic image of Surya, the sun god, has been placed.

OPPOSITE TOP A large, tranquil swimming pool with a rippling sandstone fountain lies nestled within the tree-shaded grounds of the Hotel Imperial in New Delhi.

OPPOSITE BOTTOM Secluded at the back of the extensive palace gardens, this newly constructed swimming pool at the Rambagh Palace in Jaipur is surrounded by a small grove of trees and sculpted rock formations.

ABOVE Lush purple vegetation lines the fountains that stretch from one end of Samode Bagh to the other.

RIGHT The legendary Lake Palace Hotel in Udaipur (currently known as the Taj Lake Palace) is famous for its gracious hospitality. A tented pavilion draped with white muslin and arranged around a lotus-shaped pool becomes the perfect spot for dinner.

TWO PRIVATE
HOMES IN JAIPUR

For millennia, India has been a destination of discovery for the legions of curious travelers who come to explore the rich and complex heritage of this extraordinary land. The attractions are many and varied: cultural, spiritual, academic, commercial, and more. This chapter is a brief account of the experiences of three expatriates, Mitch and Niloufar Crites and Brigitte Singh, who came to India to visit but decided to stay.

Mitch Crites, an American scholar, first came to India in 1966 to pursue his doctoral research in ancient Indian history. He soon began to work directly with a group of skilled stone carvers and master artisans and decided that he wanted to do all he could to preserve and revive their precious, endangered traditional arts and crafts. In 1986, he and his Persian wife, Niloufar, a gifted jewelry designer, moved into Bagru Haveli, a beautiful but decrepit late-eighteenth-century *haveli* courtyard home in the heart of Jaipur, near the Gate of the Moon. Over the years, they have slowly and lovingly restored the haveli, with the help of master artisans whose forefathers might very well have created the original decoration more than two hundred years ago.

Brigitte Singh came to India from her native France on a scholarship to study textiles in 1981. She, too, quickly put down roots, marrying a Rajput noble and establishing her own block-printing atelier. Guided by her academic research and inspired by traditional printing workshops still active in the village of Sanganer on the outskirts of Jaipur, Brigitte, over the years, has orchestrated a major revival of this traditional craft. Her beautiful soft furnishings, scarves, and elegant dressing gowns, block-printed with scrolling floral designs, are recognized and sold around the world.

Originally based in Jaipur, she shifted her residence and principal workshop to Amber, the hereditary seat of the maharajas of Jaipur, in the mid-1990s. Starting virtually from scratch, Brigitte designed and built a gracious two-story edifice that acts as a combined office and residence, in the middle of an old garden filled with the crumbling remains of eighteenth-century monuments. Her elegant home is located on the first floor, where she now lives with her daughter, Lilah.

PAGE 162 Raised banquettes furnished with cushions and bolsters create a comfortable and informal seating arrangement on each side of the main reception hall of Bagru Haveli, the Jaipur home of Mitch and Niloufar Crites. Bamboo blinds lined with fine cotton filter the afternoon light and add a soft glow to the room, which was once used for dance and music recitals.

PAGE 163 Master artists painted these stylized poppies and peonies on the walls of the *puja*, or worship room, at the end of the eighteenth century. They are considered to be some of the finest and most imaginative wall paintings in Jaipur.

ABOVE The Rang Mahal, or Chamber of Color, as it was traditionally known, serves as the principal reception and dining area at Bagru Haveli. The red and green cotton dhurrie carpet was designed by Niloufar Crites, and woven by local master weavers, to match the original colors of the room and to fit the space. The central focus of the room is a round dining table of green marble surrounded by antique wooden chairs.

OPPOSITE TOP LEFT An inlaid planter's chair (an English colonial lounge chair) with a glazed Persian tile in the niche above stands at the entrance to the puja. The walls of this special room are painted with flowers and the images of Hindu gods and goddesses, and the walls are covered with thin sheet of mirror.

OPPOSITE TOP RIGHT A carved white marble fountain filled with fragrant rose petals has been placed in the middle of the puja room.

OPPOSITE BOTTOM LEFT Restoration of the painted walls of Bagru Haveli continues slowly, supervised by both Niloufar and Mitch Crites. Niloufar's initials, "N.A.C.," and the date the carpet was made, 2005, have been woven into the red and green dhurrie carpet just as would have been done in the nineteenth century.

OPPOSITE BOTTOM RIGHT The white cushions and mattresses and plain bamboo chairs of the outdoor patio offer a soothing contrast to the more colorful interior of the house. An exuberant growth of palms and bougainvillea brings the feeling of a lush garden into this urban terrace.

ABOVE Large windows framed in sandstone look out on the garden and the low hills that surround Brigitte Singh's home in Jaipur. The decor of the main living area combines tradition, comfort, and elegance. Antique lamps, mirrored balls, and silver objets d'art add light and sparkle to the space. The tiled black-and-white floor is laid out in a bold chevron pattern.

OPPOSITE TOP Bamboo blinds, lined with block-printed cotton fabric designed by Brigitte Singh, cover the tall windows of the living room.

OPPOSITE BOTTOM The crumbling walls of an eighteenth-century monument behind the main residence enhance the tranquil mood of the spacious garden, which has been planted with roses, poppies, and jasmine as well as a variety of fruit-bearing trees.

TWO HAVELIS IN JAISALMER

The Hotel Shreenath Palace, perched at the top of the legendary fort of Jaisalmer in western Rajasthan, was converted to a hotel more than forty years ago, the first heritage property in the city to undergo such a transformation. Built in the sixteenth century by an early prime minister of Jaisalmer as his private residence, the traditional *haveli* courtyard house was constructed entirely from golden limestone, like that used in the fort and in major private and public buildings of the city.

Just a few narrow lanes away, the Hotel Suraj boasts a history that is similar to that of the Hotel Shreenath Palace. Originally built as a home for the finance minister of Jaisalmer state, it has only recently been converted into a heritage hotel by the owners, who can trace their family roots back more than five hundred years.

Each year hundreds of thousands of tourists from all over India and the world visit the golden city of Jaisalmer. Their patronage and appreciation of this centuries-old desert culture help ensure that heritage properties like these will never disappear.

PAGE 168 TOP A narrow arcade supported by finely carved columns of golden limestone runs along one wall of a guest bedroom. Fine muslin curtains, tie-dyed in pastel colors, soften the morning light streaming into the room.

PAGE 168 BOTTOM The elegant, sparsely decorated bedroom is furnished with a carved wooden bed. Storage space has been created out of a recess built into the stone wall above the bed.

PAGE 169 TOP Sacred to Jains across India, the sixteenth-century Parsvanath temple, located only a few hundred yards from the hotel, is open to foreigners at certain hours of the day.

PAGE 169 CENTER The stone walls of the main guest suite in the hotel are carved in high relief with male and female figures. Burgundy-colored silk used for the bedspread and cushions add further richness to the room.

PAGE 169 BOTTOM Antique brass and copper pots and vessels, part of the hotel owners' private collection, are displayed in the stone niches above the bed.

OPPOSITE TOP The restoration of the Hotel Suraj property has been conducted in an extremely sensitive manner. The early fresco paintings on the walls and arches of the bedrooms have been left totally untouched. The rooms are furnished simply, including carved wooden beds draped with red and saffron-colored spreads and cushions.

OPPOSITE BOTTOM Red ocher dots and lines have been drawn on the cupboards and the antique door, which leads onto an interior balcony. The dots and lines are coded signs placed by the owner to encourage Lord Ganesh, the remover of obstacles, and other deities to bless and protect the house throughout the year.

ABOVE This unusual bird's-eye view, seen from the uppermost balcony of the Hotel Suraj, clearly shows the forest of golden spires and domes that form the outer rooftop of the nearby Parsvanath Jain temple.

SELECTED RESOURCE GUIDE

AGRAWAL TOYS EMPORIUM
B. 1/158-A, Assi Ghat
Varanasi, Uttar Pradesh
Tel: (0542) 2311770
Wooden toys

ANOKHI
2 Tilak Marg, Ashok Nagar
Jaipur–302 001, Rajasthan
Tel: 2229247
Fabrics and clothing

EQUINOX
Gita Bhalla and Devika Surie
Ap. 3, First Floor
1 Rao Tula Ram Marg
New Delhi 110 022
Tel: 9111 2616 3518, 2616 3552
Fax: 9111 2618 5130
equinox@bol.net.in
www.equinoxtravelindia.com
Travel agency

FABINDIA
C-69, Sarojini Marg, C-Scheme
Jaipur–302 001, Rajasthan
Tel: 5115991,2
www.fabindia.com
Fabrics and clothing

HASIN MOHAMMED
H.M. Textiles
K. 52/52 Dulligaddi (behind Yamuna Talkies)
Varanasi–221001, Uttar Pradesh
Brocade weaving

KRITI GALLERY
Nandita and Navneet Raman
Raja Sir Motichand Road
Mahmoor Ganj
Varanasi–10, Uttar Pradesh
Tel: (0542) 2363350
www.kritigallery.com
Art

NEERJA INTERNATIONAL INC.
Leela Bordia
S-19 Bhawani Singh Road, C-Scheme Ext.
Jaipur–302 001, Rajasthan
Tel: 2224395
Blue pottery

SEWA/SELF-EMPLOYED WOMEN'S ASSOCIATION
SEWA Reception Center
Bhadra
Ahmedabad–380 001, Gujarat
Tel: 25506444
www.sewa.org
Women's organization

THOLIA'S KUBER
Tholia Building, M.I. Road
Jaipur–302 001, Rajasthan
Tel: 2377416
Jewelry

NEAR RIGHT A bustling sari shop in Jodhpur.

FAR RIGHT Western-style mannequins wearing glittering *dupattas* (long scarves), in a shop window in Jaipur.

hotel directory

ALSISAR HAVELI
Sansar Chandra Road
District Jaipur
Jaipur–302 001, Rajasthan
Tel: 91 (0)141 2368290/2364685
Fax: 91 (0)141 2364652
alsisar@alsisar.com
www.alsisar.com

ALSISAR MAHAL
District Jhunjhunu
Alsisar–Rajasthan
Tel: 91 (0)1595 275271-2
alsisar@alsisar.com
www.alsisar.com

AMAR MAHAL
District Tikamgarh
Orchha–472 246, Madhya Pradesh
Tel: 91 (0)7680 252102/252202
Fax: 91 (0)7680 252203
alsisar@alsisar.com
www.alsisar.com

BHANWAR NIWAS
Rampuria Street
District Bikaner
Bikaner–334 005, Rajasthan
Tel: 91 (0)151 2529323/2201043
Fax: 91 (0)151 2200880
bhanwarniwas@rediffmail.com
www.bhanwarniwas.com

CASTLE MANDAWA
Sansar Chandra Road
District Jhunjhunu
Mandawa–302 001, Rajasthan
Tel: 91 (0)141 371194/2374112
Fax: 91 (0)159 2223171
reservations@castlemandawa.com
www.castlemandawa.com

DEOGARH MAHAL
Deogarh Madaria
District Rajsamand
Deogarh–313 331, Rajasthan
Tel: 91 (0)2904 252777
Fax: 91 (0)2904 253333
info@deogarhmahal.com
www.deogarhmahal.com

DEVIGARH FORT PALACE
District Rajsamand
Village Delwara–313 001, Rajasthan
Tel: 91 (0)2953 289211-20
Fax: 91 (0)2953 289357
devigarh@deviresorts.com
www.deviresorts.com

FORT RAJWADA
Jodhpur-Barmer Link Road
Jaisalmer–345 001, Rajasthan
Tel: 91 (0)2992 253233/253533
Fax: 91 (0)2992 253733
sales@fortrajwada.com
www.fortrajwada.com

HOTEL MANDAWA HAVELI
Near Sonthaliya Gate Mandawa
District Jhunjhunu
Mandawa–333 704, Rajasthan
Tel: 91 (0)1592 223088
Fax: 91 (0)1592 224060
hotelmandawahaveli@yahoo.com
www.hotelmandawa.free.fr

HOTEL SHREENATH HAVELI
398, inside Jaisalmer Fort,
near Jain Temple
District Jaisalmer
Jaisalmer–345 001, Rajasthan
Tel: 91 (0)2992 252907
shreenath52907@hotmail.com
www.shreenathpalace.com

HOTEL SURAJ HAVELI
222, inside Jaisalmer Fort,
near Jain Temple
District Jaisalmer
Jaisalmer–345 001, Rajasthan
Tel: 91 (0)2992 251623
Fax: 91 (0)2992 253614
hotelsurajjaisalmer@hotmail.com

THE IMPERIAL
Janpath–110 001, New Delhi
Tel: 91 (0)11 23341234/41501234
Fax: 91 (0)11 23342255
luxury@theimperialindia.com
www.theimperialindia.com

KHIMSAR FORT
District Nagaur
Khimsar–341 025, Rajasthan
Tel: 91 (0)1585 262345-9
Fax: 91 (0)1585 262228
khimsar_jp1@sancharnet.in
www.khimsarfort.com

KUCHAMAN FORT
District Nagaur
Kuchaman–341 508, Rajasthan
Tel: 91 (0)1586 220884
Fax: 91 (0)1586 220882
sales@kuchamanfort.com
www.kuchamanfort.com

LALLGARH PALACE
Dr. Karni Singhji Road
District Bikaner
Bikaner–334 001, Rajasthan
Tel: 91 (0)151 2540201-7
Fax: 91 (0)151 2523963
info:lallgarhpalace.com
www.lallgarhpalace.com

LAXMI NIWAS PALACE
Dr. Karni Singhji Road
District Bikaner
Bikaner–334 001, Rajasthan
Tel: 91 (0)151 2202777/2521188
Fax: 91 (0)151 2521487
reservation@laxminiwaspalace.com
www.laxminiwaspalace.com

LAXMI VILAS PALACE HOTEL
Kakaji Kothi, Old Agra Road
District Bharatpur
Bharatpur–321 001, Rajasthan
Tel: 91 (0)5644 223523/231199
Fax: 91 (0)5644 225259
reservations@laxmivilas.com
www.laxmivilas.com

NAHAGARH PALACE HOTEL
Ranthambhor Road
District Sawai Madhopur
Sawai Madhopur–322 001, Rajasthan
Tel: 91 (0)7462 252281-3
Fax: 91 (0)7642 251246
alsisar@alsisar.com
www.alsisar.com

NARAIN NIWAS PALACE
Kanota Bagh, Narain Singh Road
District Jaipur
Jaipur–302 004, Rajasthan
Tel: 91 (0)141 2561291/2563448
Fax: 91 (0)141 2561045
kanota@sancharnet.in
www.narainniwas.com

NEEMRANA FORT-PALACE
District Alwar
Village Neemrana–301 705, Rajasthan
Tel: 91 (0)1494 246006-8
Fax: 91 (0)1494 246005
sales@neemranahotels.com
www.neemranahotels.com

OBEROI AMARVILAS
Taj East Gate
Agra–282 001, Uttar Pradesh
Tel: 91 (0)562 2231515
Fax: 91 (0)562 2231516
reservatioins@oberoi-amarvilas.com
www.oberoihotels.com

OBEROI RAJVILAS
Goner Road
District Jaipur
Jaipur–303 012, Rajasthan
Tel: 91(0)141 2680101
Fax: 91(0)141 2680202
reservations@oberoi-rajvilas.com
www.oberoihotels.com

OBEROI UDAIVILAS
Haridasji ki Magri
District Udaipur
Udaipur–313 001, Rajasthan
Tel: 91 (0)294 2433300
Fax: 91 (0)294 2433200
reservations@oberoi-udaivilas.com
www.oberoihotels.com

PHOOL MAHAL PALACE
District Kishangarh
Kishangarh–305 802, Rajasthan
Tel: 91 (0)463 247405/247505
Fax: 91 (0)463 247505
phoolmahalpalace@yahoo.com
www.royalkishangarh.com

RAJ NIWAS PALACE
District Dholpur
Dholpur–Rajasthan
Tel: 91 (0)5642 220216
Fax: 91 (0)5642 221271
Mob: 91 (0)9414027979
info@dholpurpalace.com
www.dholpurpalace.com

RAMBAGH PALACE
Bhawani Singh Road
District Jaipur
Jaipur–302 005, Rajasthan
Tel: 91 (0)141 2211919
Fax: 91 (0)141 2385098
rambagh.jaipur@tajhotels.com
www.tajhotels.com

SAMODE HAVELI
Gangapole
District Jaipur
Jaipur–302 002, Rajasthan
Tel: 91 (0)141 2632407/2632370
Fax: 91 (0)141 2631397
reservations@samode.com
www.samode.com

**SAMODE PALACE
AND SAMODE BAGH**
District Jaipur
Samode Town–303 806, Rajasthan
Tel: 91 (0)1423 240014/240023
Fax: 91 (0)141 2632370/2631397
reservations@samode.com
www.samode.com

SEENGH SAGAR
Deogarh Madaria
District Rajsamand
Deogarh–313 331, Rajasthan
Tel: 91 (0)2904 252777
Fax: 91 (0)2904 253333
info@deogarhmahal.com
www.deogarhmahal.com

SHIV NIWAS PALACE
The City Palace Complex
District Udaipur
Udaipur–313 001, Rajasthan
Tel: 91 (0)294 2528016-19
Fax: 91 (0)284 2528006/2528012
crs@udaipur.hrhindia.com
www.hrhindia.com

TAJ LAKE PALACE
Pichola Lake
P.O. Box No. 5
District Udaipur
Udaipur–313 001, Rajasthan
Tel: 91 (0)294 2528800
Fax: 91 (0)294 2528700
lakepalace.udaipur@tajhotels.com
www.tajhotels.com

UDAI KOTHI
Hanuman Ghat
Udaipur–313 001, Rajasthan
Tel: 91 (0)294 2432810-12
Fax: 91 (0)294 2430412
udaikothi@yahoo.com
www.udaikothi.com

UMAID BHAWAN PALACE
District Jodhpur
Jodhpur–342 006, Rajasthan
Tel: 91 (0)1291 2510101-5
Fax: 91 (0)1291 2510100
ubpresv.jodh@tajhotels.com
www.tajhotels.com

acknowledgments

We extend our deepest thanks to the many women, men, children, artisans, painters, dancers, and musicians in India who allowed us to photograph them and their work. Their zest for life, artistic skills, welcoming spirit, and curiosity have left an indelible mark of joy on our memories. We would also like to honor the original builders and artists, long deceased, whose work we photographed and whose skills and techniques continue to excite and inspire us. We would like to thank Gita Bhalla and Devika Surie at Equinox for their invaluable assistance in organizing our travel and accommodations. Many thanks to Hugh Levick for his invaluable assistance, Anne Laval for her constant support, and Niloufar Afshar-Crites for her generous and warm hospitality in Jaipur. Thanks also to Navneet and Nandita Raman and their family for introducing us to the world of textiles in Varanasi. We are grateful to Nanine and Bert Fox for their wonderful teaching and indispensable advice and to Pauline Van Lynden for her visual inspiration and generosity.

Additional thanks go to a number of individuals who generously gave their assistance, time, and advice. They are Bimla Poddar, Brigitte Singh, Caroline Desouza, Mohammad Lateef, Varun Seth, Azmina Kanji, Aman Nath, and Francis Wacziarg. Many thanks are due to our agent, Sarah Jane Freymann, for her continued commitment and dedication. Finally, this book would not have been possible without the guidance, insight, and support of our editor, Lisa Campbell; our copy editor, Karen Stein; and the team at Chronicle Books: Steve Kim, production coordinator; Vanessa Dina, art director; and Jennifer Sparkman and Evan Hulka, managing editorial staff. Thank you.

PAGE 175 A painted wooden image of Lord Ganesha, Remover of Obstacles, carved with five heads.

RIGHT A young performer from the Bhopa community wearing traditional clothing.